Acknowledgments

This book is the result of more than twenty five years of reading, studying, listening, writing, and lecturing.

Dr. Neji Ben Hadj Tahar Mzoughi and I are deeply indebted to our spouses, Amina and Widad, respectively, for their wholehearted support and encouragement. They created the right intellectual environment, allowing us to spend many evenings in conversation, discussion, and analysis of new ideas, articles, and books. The Quran was always present, guiding our thinking without ever diminishing our personal autonomy and agency.

I am very thankful to my friends—Hatem ElGabri, Esq., Dr. Qais Mekki, Dr. Issam Dairanieh, and Dr. Walid Awni—as well as my daughter Yasmeen and Neji's son Ibrahim, for their invaluable and meaningful input. Each of them contributed according to their professional background and life experience.

Words cannot fully express my tremendous gratitude to my immediate and extended family members—both those who have passed and those still with us—who have encouraged me in all my endeavors. This book is a simple and modest gift to them in return.

About the Arabic Author

Dr. Neji Ben Hadj Tahar Mzoughi is a scholar whose academic journey bridges the natural sciences, social sciences, and the humanities. He began his studies at the University of the Center in Monastir, Tunisia, earning a bachelor's degree in physics after completing coursework in mathematics, physics, and chemistry. Following his undergraduate studies, he taught physics and chemistry at Ksar Hellal High School before moving to Canada to further his education.

In Canada, Dr. Neji pursued graduate studies at the University of Quebec in Montreal, earning a Master's degree in Atmospheric Sciences. He then shifted his focus to the social sciences, completing a Ph.D. in Sociology with distinction at the same university. His doctoral dissertation examined the rise and fall of civilizations, offering an original extension of the Khaldunian model of civilizational dynamics.

For more than thirty years, Dr. Neji has devoted himself to consultations, discussions, and seminars, searching for a methodology to understand the challenge of direction and purpose in human life. He has worked to establish foundational principles that transform this quest into a science—one that makes human action virtuous at both the individual and collective levels. His work is rooted in the Glorious Qur'an, which introduces itself as guidance and mercy for all of humanity and for all times (see, for example, 25:1, 21:107, 34:28, 7:158). Dr. Neji's work seeks to crystallize a Qur'anic vision that serves as a compass for achieving this purpose, guiding human action to be righteous and good, led by a free individual who knows God and is conscious of her/his role in existence.

On a more personal note, after his journey in Canada, Dr. Neji moved to the United States, where he has worked as a software engineer and now serves as a consultant in the IT field in Chicago.

His intellectual interests span Qur'anic studies and the philosophy of history. He is the author of *Man and the Quran: An Introduction to the Science of Guidance*, published by Dar Al-Fikr in Damascus, and he occasionally lectures on these topics at international conferences.

Dr. Neji resides in the United States with his wife and three children.

About the English Translator and Adaptor

Dr. Walid Fayez Khayr is a medical graduate of the American University of Beirut, class of 1985. In 1988, he moved to Chicago, Illinois, where he completed his fellowship in Infectious Disease at the University of Illinois at Chicago. He is board-certified in both Internal Medicine and Infectious Disease, and currently serves as a Clinical Professor of Medicine at Rosalind Franklin University of Medicine and Science / The Chicago Medical School.

Dr. Khayr is the author of numerous scientific articles in the field of Infectious Disease, published in peer-reviewed journals. While he remains active in clinical practice and academic medicine, Dr. Khayr also has a deep interest in the role of religion in social life. He has expressed this interest through Friday sermons, lectures, seminars, book-club conversations, weekly online discussions of Quranic passages, and interfaith dialogues at various institutions and places of worship.

Dr. Khayr resides in the United States with his wife and four children.

Contents

How to Use This Book 11

Author's Note of Appreciation 12

Prologue 14

    Encountering a Transformative Vision 14

Chapter One 17

    Action, Direction, and Qibla 17

        Chapter Summary (Proposal) 17

        1. The "Action" and Its "Direction" 17

        2. The Universe: Reference Validating Action, Silent on Direction 21

        3. The Divine Guidance: The Reference for Ethical Direction (Hudā) of Human Action 22

        4. Qibla (قبلة) 25

Chapter Two 31

    "Ayah": The Expression in The Cosmic Vision of Quran 31

        Chapter Summary (Proposal) 31

        What is a Cosmic Vision? 31

        "Ayah" as a Quranic Expression 31

        Contexts of "Ayah" in the Quran 32

        "Ayah" in The Universe 33

        "Ayah" in Quran 35

        "Ayah" in Human History 35

        The Triad: Universe, Revelation, and History 36

        The Divine System of Creation and Command 38

- Chapter Three 40
  - The Beautiful Names of God 40
    - A Conceptual and Ethical Framework 40
    - Knowing God Through His Beautiful Names 40
    - The Power and Significance of Naming 41
    - The Concept of I'tibar in Approaching the Beautiful Names of God 43
    - God-Human Relationship 44
    - The Concept of Ibada 47
    - High Values Derived from the Beautiful Names of God 48
- Chapter Four 52
  - The Universe in The Cosmic Vision of the Quran 52
    - Chapter Summary (Proposal) 52
    - Creation of the Universe: Six Periods 52
    - The Universe as the Reference for Human Action 53
    - How the Universe is Presented to Humans 53
    - The Organic Relationship Between Humans and the Universe 58
    - Diversity in the Universe 59
    - Creation in Pairs 61
    - Definition: The Human Project 61
- Chapter Five 63
  - The Name "Quran": A Novel Arabic Expression 63
    - Chapter Summary (Proposal) 63
    - Types of Expressions in Quran 63

- The Etymology of the Expression "Quran" 65
- Structure and function of Quran 66
- The Expression of "Kalimat" 67
- The Expression "Umm Al-Kitab" 68
- The Expression of "Furqan" 68
- "Tasdeeq" and "Hymana" 69
- "Mutashabihat" and "Muhkamat" 69
- "Tafseer" and "Taaweel" 71

Chapter Six 77
- The Human in The Cosmic Vision of Quran 77
  - Chapter Summary (Proposal) 77
  - Names and Expressions for Human Beings 77
  - Stages of the Human Journey in the Quranic Vision 83

Chapter Seven 87
- Quranic Expressions: A Tool to Study The Emergence of Moral Classes 87
  - Moral Classes in the Quran 87
  - Progression of Virtues and Added Values 88
  - Immoral Classes and Social Illnesses 90
  - Habits and the Formation of Culture 93
  - The Prophetic Model of Moral Education 95

Chapter Eight 100
- The Evolution of Umma: Quranic Expressions as a Roadmap 100
  - The Sun and the Day: A Quranic Analogy 100
  - The Prophet as "Siraj" 101

    The Meaning and Evolution of "Umma" 102

    Crisis and the Quranic Recipe for Rescue 105

    Returning to Fitra and High Values 108

Chapter Nine 113

    Challenge and Response: Why is "Giving" a Different Expression in the Quran? 113

        Giving as Self-Purification: The Early Challenge 113

        Giving in Medina: Social Cohesion and Leadership 114

        Nifaq and Infaq: The Internal Challenge 116

        External Threats: Giving as Struggle 117

        Conclusion: The Dynamic Language of Giving 117

Chapter Ten 118

    Human History: The Moral and The Morale 118

    Prophetic Guidance and Lessons from History 118

    Four Functions of History in the Quran 119

    History as a Laboratory and the Quranic Approach 121

    Surah Al-Rum: A Case Study in History and Morale 122

Epilogue 129

    The Imperative of a Science of Guidance 129

    The Foundations of a New Discipline 129

    The Living Scripture and Its Future 130

Glossary of Key Terms 131

How to Use This Book

This book is designed to guide readers from foundational concepts to advanced applications of the Quranic cosmic vision. Each chapter begins with a concise summary and is organized with clear subheadings for ease of navigation. Key Arabic terms and expressions are explained in the glossary at the end of the book, allowing readers to deepen their understanding of essential concepts as they progress.

Readers are encouraged to engage actively with the material:
- Reflect on the tables, diagrams, and visual frameworks provided throughout the chapters.
- Use the book for both individual study and group discussion, drawing connections between the Quranic vision and contemporary challenges.
- Refer to the glossary whenever unfamiliar terms arise, and revisit earlier chapters as needed to reinforce understanding.

This book is suitable for both general readers and academic audiences. Whether you are approaching the Quran for the first time or seeking to expand your scholarly engagement, the structure and resources provided are intended to support a transformative reading experience.

Author's Note of Appreciation

It is with great pleasure and deep gratitude that I extend my heartfelt congratulations to Dr. Walid Khayr for his outstanding work in translating and adapting my book, Man and The Quran: An Introduction to The Science of Guidance (معالم الإنسان والقرآن، علم الوجهة), for the English-speaking world. Throughout his careful and thoughtful engagement with my original Arabic text, Dr. Walid has demonstrated both scholarly rigor and a profound sensitivity to the spirit and intent of my work.

As the author, I have reviewed his translation and adaptation of the ten chapters presented in this volume. I am pleased to affirm that Dr. Walid has remained true to the core ideas, arguments, and vision articulated in the original Arabic edition. His adaptation is not a mere literal translation, but a creative and faithful rendering that preserves the integrity of my thought while making it accessible and resonant for a new audience. The structure, conceptual depth, and intellectual ambition of the original work have been maintained throughout, and I am gratified to see my ideas so accurately and elegantly conveyed.

Dr. Walid's scholarly integrity and commitment to clarity have ensured that the essence of 'Ilm al-Wajhah—the Science of Guidance—emerges with renewed vitality in this English edition. I am confident that this work will serve as a valuable resource for both general readers and specialists, and that it will contribute meaningfully to contemporary discussions on the Quran, Islamic thought, and the philosophy of guidance.

I thank Dr. Walid for his dedication, his intellectual partnership, and his friendship. May this book inspire further dialogue and discovery, and may it serve as a bridge between cultures and traditions in the ongoing quest for understanding and guidance.

Dr. Neji Ben Hadj Tahar Mzoughi
Author, Man and The Quran: An Introduction to The Science of Guidance

Prologue

Encountering a Transformative Vision

My enduring fascination with transformative ideas led me, by God's grace, to encounter Dr. Neji Ben Hadj Tahar Mzoughi twenty-five years ago. From our first meeting, I recognized him as an exceptional scholar whose intellect bridges the sciences and humanities—a rare polymath equipped to reimagine Quranic engagement for our time.

Dr. Neji's interdisciplinary journey laid the groundwork for his unique perspective:

• Born and raised in Tunisia, he completed undergraduate studies in mathematics, physics, and chemistry.

• He continued his academic pursuits in Montréal, Canada, earning a Master's in Metrology from Université du Québec, followed by a PhD in Sociology. His doctoral thesis interrogated Ibn Khaldun's model of civilizational dynamics, foreshadowing his later work on Quranic historiography and the rise and fall of civilizations.

In 2021, Dr. Neji published Man and The Quran: An Introduction to The Science of Guidance (in Arabic) (الإنسان والقرآن، معالم علم الوجهة). The book's revolutionary framework transcends traditional exegetical approaches, offering a fresh and comprehensive vision of the Quran's guidance for humanity. Translating such a work into English is a daunting task, even for professionals. Rather than attempt a literal translation, I chose to craft an adaptation—distilling Dr. Neji's seminal ideas and presenting them in a way that would resonate with the English-speaking world and ensure their global impact.

The central challenge was structural: how to unify his "cosmic vision" of the Quran into a coherent narrative. The solution emerged organically—the Quran's own conceptual architecture became the organizing spine of this work.

The book unfolds as follows:

- Chapters 1–3 establish the foundations:
    1. The human triad—Action, Direction, and Qibla (spiritual orientation).
    2. The Quran's cosmic framework.
    3. Its transcendent anchor: al-Asmā' al-Ḥusnā (The Beautiful Names of God).
- Chapters 4–6 explore the cosmic triad:
    1. The Universe (Divine creation),
    2. Revelation (Divine communication),
    3. The Human (Divine purpose).
- Chapters 7–10 map societal transformation:
    7. The evolution of the Umma as a responsive community.
    8. Quranic economies of "giving" across historical challenges.
    9. The emergence of moral hierarchies (rather than power structures) within the Umma.
    10. The Quranic approach to history and the methodology that liberates believers from the "superpower prison."

The work concludes by synthesizing these strands into recommendations for future research, launching Dr. Neji's proposed ʿIlm al-Wijhah (Science of Guidance: علم الوجهة) into contemporary scholarly discourse.

This book is intended for both the general reader and the academic community. It aims to make accessible the profound insights of Dr. Neji's scholarship, while also providing a rigorous conceptual framework for those engaged in the study of Quranic thought, Islamic civilization, and the philosophy of history.

Chapter One

Action, Direction, and Qibla

Chapter Summary (Proposal)

This chapter introduces three foundational Quranic concepts—Fi'l (action), Wijha (direction), and Qibla (ultimate goal)—and explores how the Quran distinguishes between the mechanics of action, the ethical orientation of action, and the ultimate purpose that unifies human endeavor. Through scriptural examples and analysis, the chapter demonstrates how direction and intention transform the moral value of identical acts, and how the Qibla serves as a civilizational compass for the Muslim community.

This book advances the cosmic vision derived from the Quran as proposed by Dr. Neji, alongside its sustaining conceptual and ethical framework. As foundational preparation, this chapter distinguishes three pivotal Quranic concepts:

- Fi'l (فعل): Human action
- Wijha (وجهة): The direction orienting action
- Qibla (قبلة): The ultimate goal

1. The "Action" and Its "Direction"

The Quran repeatedly decouples action from its direction—demonstrating that identical deeds acquire divergent moral valuations based on their orientation. Consider food consumption:

- Eating slaughtered livestock (sheep, cattle, or camel) may be permissible (ḥalāl) or forbidden (ḥarām) solely based on whether God's Name consecrated the act of slaughter.

Direction transforms the act's essence: The same physical deed becomes sacred or profane through its spiritual intentionality.

This principle permeates Quranic ethics. The text consistently elevates wijha (direction) as the ethical compass that:
- Determines an action's moral weight,
- Transcends mere outward form,
- Anchors human conduct in divine consciousness.

"So, eat of (meats) on which Allah's name has been pronounced, if you have faith in His Signs" [6:118]

فَكُلُوا مِمَّا ذُكِرَ ٱسْمُ ٱللَّهِ عَلَيْهِ إِن كُنتُم بِـَٔايَـٰتِهِۦ مُؤْمِنِينَ

"Eat not of (meats) on which Allah's name has not been pronounced: that would be impiety" [6:121]

وَلَا تَأْكُلُوا مِمَّا لَمْ يُذْكَرِ ٱسْمُ ٱللَّهِ عَلَيْهِ وَإِنَّهُۥ لَفِسْقٌ

Another example: The fruits of dates and grapes can be used for good sustenance or used to make alcoholic drinks that are associated with bad effects on human physical and mental health:

"And from the fruit of the date palm and the vine, you get out wholesome drink and food: behold, in this also is a Sign for those who are wise." [16:67]

وَمِن ثَمَرَٰتِ ٱلنَّخِيلِ وَٱلْأَعْنَـٰبِ تَتَّخِذُونَ مِنْهُ سَكَرًا وَرِزْقًا حَسَنًا ۗ إِنَّ فِى ذَٰلِكَ لَـَٔايَةً لِّقَوْمٍ يَعْقِلُونَ

The Quran also differentiates between giving in the way of God versus giving in order to obstruct the way to God. The difference is clearly in the direction:

"And spend of your substance in the cause of Allah, and make not your own hands contribute to (your) destruction; but do good; for Allah loves those who do good" [2:195]

وَأَنفِقُوا فِى سَبِيلِ ٱللَّهِ وَلَا تُلْقُوا بِأَيْدِيكُمْ إِلَى ٱلتَّهْلُكَةِ ۛ وَأَحْسِنُوٓا ۛ إِنَّ ٱللَّهَ يُحِبُّ ٱلْمُحْسِنِينَ

"The Unbelievers spend their wealth to hinder (men) from the path of Allah, and so will they continue to spend; but in the end they will have regrets and sighs; at length they will be overcome: and the Unbelievers will be gathered together to Hell" [8:36]

إِنَّ ٱلَّذِينَ كَفَرُوا۟ يُنفِقُونَ أَمْوَٰلَهُمْ لِيَصُدُّوا۟ عَن سَبِيلِ ٱللَّهِ ۚ فَسَيُنفِقُونَهَا ثُمَّ تَكُونُ عَلَيْهِمْ حَسْرَةً ثُمَّ يُغْلَبُونَ ۗ وَٱلَّذِينَ كَفَرُوٓا۟ إِلَىٰ جَهَنَّمَ يُحْشَرُونَ

Indeed, the first revealed Quranic verse commands humans to read – but not any reading; to read while keeping in mind the name of God who creates, so human reading becomes creative:

"Read in the name of your Lord and Cherisher, Who created" [96:1]

ٱقْرَأْ بِٱسْمِ رَبِّكَ ٱلَّذِى خَلَقَ

Humans move and act in this world to sustain life. Yet with every action, they face the challenge of its direction or meaning. The Quran captures this in the first incident in human history where Adam's two sons (PBUH) confronted this directional challenge in the complete passage:

"Recite to them the truth of the story of the two sons of Adam. Behold! they each presented a sacrifice: it was accepted from one, but not from the other. Said the latter: "Be sure I will slay you." "Surely," said the former, "Allah does accept the sacrifice of those who are righteous. If you do stretch your hand against me, to slay me, it is not for me to stretch my hand against you to slay you: for I do fear Allah, the Cherisher of the worlds. For me, I intend to let you draw on yourself my sin as well as yours, for you will be among the companions of the Fire, and that is the reward of those who do wrong. The (selfish) soul of the other led him to the murder of his brother: he murdered him, and became (himself) one of the lost ones. Then Allah sent a raven, who scratched the ground, to show him how to hide the shame of his brother. Woe is me! said he, was I not even able to be like this raven, and to hide the shame of my brother? Then he became full of regrets." [5:27-31]

وَاتْلُ عَلَيْهِمْ نَبَأَ ابْنَيْ آدَمَ بِالْحَقِّ إِذْ قَرَّبَا قُرْبَانًا فَتُقُبِّلَ مِنْ أَحَدِهِمَا وَلَمْ يُتَقَبَّلْ مِنَ الْآخَرِ قَالَ لَأَقْتُلَنَّكَ ۖ قَالَ إِنَّمَا يَتَقَبَّلُ اللَّهُ مِنَ الْمُتَّقِينَ

لَئِنْ بَسَطْتَ إِلَيَّ يَدَكَ لِتَقْتُلَنِي مَا أَنَا بِبَاسِطٍ يَدِيَ إِلَيْكَ لِأَقْتُلَكَ ۖ إِنِّي أَخَافُ اللَّهَ رَبَّ الْعَالَمِينَ

إِنِّي أُرِيدُ أَنْ تَبُوءَ بِإِثْمِي وَإِثْمِكَ فَتَكُونَ مِنْ أَصْحَابِ النَّارِ ۚ وَذَٰلِكَ جَزَاءُ الظَّالِمِينَ

فَطَوَّعَتْ لَهُ نَفْسُهُ قَتْلَ أَخِيهِ فَقَتَلَهُ فَأَصْبَحَ مِنَ الْخَاسِرِينَ

فَبَعَثَ اللَّهُ غُرَابًا يَبْحَثُ فِي الْأَرْضِ لِيُرِيَهُ كَيْفَ يُوَارِي سَوْءَةَ أَخِيهِ ۚ قَالَ يَا وَيْلَتَىٰ أَعَجَزْتُ أَنْ أَكُونَ مِثْلَ هَٰذَا الْغُرَابِ فَأُوَارِيَ سَوْءَةَ أَخِي ۖ فَأَصْبَحَ مِنَ النَّادِمِينَ

Their responses differed: One refused to kill and was martyred; the other committed fratricide. Though the murderer couldn't perform the simple act of burying his brother, he committed an atrocity. This illustrates that corrupting an action's direction is far more dangerous than omitting or delaying the action itself.

Example	Act (Fi'l)	Direction (Wijha)	Outcome
Slaughter	Killing an animal	With God's name	Halal (permissible)
Slaughter	Killing an animal	Without God's name	Haram (forbidden)
Dates/Grapes	Using fruit	For food	Wholesome

Dates/Grapes	Using fruit	For alcohol	Harmful
Charity	Giving wealth	For God's cause	Rewarded
Charity	Giving wealth	To obstruct God's way	Condemned

2. The Universe: Reference Validating Action, Silent on Direction

Human actions (fi'l/فعل) are empirically validated through the Universe—our ultimate reference for practical efficacy. We observe actions succeeding only when aligned with cosmic laws. Yet while the Universe arbitrates mechanical outcomes (e.g., a bridge's stability), it remains silent on moral direction (wijha/وجهة). This duality demands vigilant discernment: every action requires ethical orientation to advance life toward its ultimate purpose (qibla).

The Universe's Jurisdiction and Limits
Consider structural engineering:
- Building a stable house validates adherence to physical laws (fi'l achieved).
- But the Universe judges neither intent nor end-use: shelter for refugees or a barracks for tyranny.

This silence necessitates transcendent guidance. Though trial-and-error hones technical skill, divorcing action from ethical direction corrupts its essence:

The Knife Paradox
The identical fi'l (cutting) yields antithetical realities through tawjīh (توجيه):

- Direction A (Sustenance): Preparing nourishment (cutting bread/fruit).
- Direction B (Violation): Inflicting harm (wounding/killing).

Same mechanics, diametrically opposed moral trajectories.

Thus, the Universe governs how actions function, but Revelation defines why they matter. Cosmic laws enable fiʿl, but wijha—the ethical vector of human will—flows from divine instruction.

3. The Divine Guidance: The Reference for Ethical Direction (Hudā) of Human Action

Divine Revelation establishes itself as the ultimate reference for hudā (هدى)—guidance that ethically orients human action (tawjīh/توجيه). This foundational role is demonstrated in humanity's primordial narrative:

"We said: 'O Adam! Dwell with your mate in Paradise; eat freely thereof where you will, but approach not this tree lest you become wrongdoers.'" [2:35]

وَقُلْنَا يَٰٓـَٔادَمُ ٱسْكُنْ أَنتَ وَزَوْجُكَ ٱلْجَنَّةَ وَكُلَا مِنْهَا رَغَدًا حَيْثُ شِئْتُمَا وَلَا تَقْرَبَا هَٰذِهِ ٱلشَّجَرَةَ فَتَكُونَا مِنَ ٱلظَّٰلِمِينَ

In this elevated state:
- All sustenance was permitted except one tree.
- Guidance took the form of explicit boundaries ("do"/"do not")—establishing Revelation as humanity's first ethical reference.

Yet Divine warning accompanied this freedom:

"Then Satan whispered to them to expose their nakedness, which had been hidden from them. He said: 'Your Lord forbade this tree only lest you become angels or immortals.'" [7:20]

فَوَسْوَسَ لَهُمَا ٱلشَّيْطَٰنُ لِيُبْدِيَ لَهُمَا مَا وُۥرِىَ عَنْهُمَا مِن سَوْءَٰتِهِمَا وَقَالَ مَا نَهَىٰكُمَا رَبُّكُمَا عَنْ هَٰذِهِ ٱلشَّجَرَةِ إِلَّآ أَن تَكُونَا مَلَكَيْنِ أَوْ تَكُونَا مِنَ ٱلْخَٰلِدِينَ

Here, humanity confronted a pivotal truth: Even in perfection, moral direction requires conscious alignment with Divine reference—a choice vulnerable to distortion.

Adam and his mate thus became conscious of their freedom to choose – a freedom intrinsically bound to responsibility and accountability. When they began earthly life, Divine communication transformed:

"Then his Lord chose him (for His grace), accepted his repentance, and gave him guidance." [20:122]

ثُمَّ ٱجْتَبَٰهُ رَبُّهُۥ فَتَابَ عَلَيْهِ وَهَدَىٰ

The command now took the form of guidance (hudā), empowering humans as agents who must:
- Think (tafakkur/تفكر)
- Analyze (tadabbur/تدبر)
- Discern direction (tawjīh/توجيه)

"[This is] guidance for those mindful of Allah." [2:2]

هُدًى لِّلْمُتَّقِينَ

Divine guidance does not negate human agency but elevates it, providing the moral compass to direct (yuwajjihu/يوجه) actions toward their ultimate purpose.

The Covenant of Continuous Guidance
Humans were thus promised perpetual access to this directional reference:

"We said: 'Descend, all of you! Then when guidance comes to you from Me, whoever follows it, there will be no fear for them, nor will they grieve.'" [2:38]

قُلْنَا ٱهْبِطُوا۟ مِنْهَا جَمِيعًا ۖ فَإِمَّا يَأْتِيَنَّكُم مِّنِّى هُدًى فَمَن تَبِعَ هُدَاىَ فَلَا خَوْفٌ عَلَيْهِمْ وَلَا هُمْ يَحْزَنُونَ

Two phases mark humanity's relationship with hudā:
- Era 1 (Passive Reception): Guidance given unsought (Adam's descendants).
- Era 2 (Active Seeking): Prophet Ibrahim (PBUH) pioneered conscious recourse to the Divine reference:

"When he saw the moon rising, he said, 'This is my Lord.' But when it set, he declared, 'Unless my Lord guides me, I will certainly be among the misguided!'" [6:77]

فَلَمَّا رَءَا ٱلْقَمَرَ بَازِغًا قَالَ هَٰذَا رَبِّى ۖ فَلَمَّآ أَفَلَ قَالَ لَئِن لَّمْ يَهْدِنِى رَبِّى لَأَكُونَنَّ مِنَ ٱلْقَوْمِ ٱلضَّآلِّينَ

Al-Najdayn: Dual Pathways of Guidance
Hudā (هدى) invariably references al-ṣirāṭ al-mustaqīm (ٱلصِّرَٰطَ ٱلْمُسْتَقِيمَ). This demands re-examining Surah Al-Balad's pivotal verse:

"And We showed him the two pathways?" [90:10]

وَهَدَيْنَٰهُ ٱلنَّجْدَيْنِ (10)

Key Inference: Beyond "Good vs. Evil"
The "two pathways" signify distinct guidance references:
1. Guidance for Action (Fi'l/فعل)
   Reference: The Universe (validates mechanics: how to build, plant, heal).
2. Guidance for Direction (Wijhat al-Fi'l/وجهة الفعل)

Reference: Revelation (validates ethics: why and for whom actions are done).

Validation: The "Steep Path" (Al-'Aqabah)
This duality is proven by verses 11-17 delineating social actions directed by higher values:

"But he has not attempted the steep path. And what can make you know what is the steep path? It is freeing a slave, or feeding on a day of famine an orphaned relative or a poor person in distress. Then he becomes one of those who believe, urge one another to patience, and urge one another to compassion." [90:11-17]

فَلَا ٱقْتَحَمَ ٱلْعَقَبَةَ (11) وَمَا أَدْرَىٰكَ مَا ٱلْعَقَبَةُ (12) فَكُّ رَقَبَةٍ (13) أَوْ إِطْعَامٌ فِى يَوْمٍ ذِى مَسْغَبَةٍ (14) يَتِيمًا ذَا مَقْرَبَةٍ (15) أَوْ مِسْكِينًا ذَا مَتْرَبَةٍ (16) ثُمَّ كَانَ مِنَ ٱلَّذِينَ ءَامَنُوا۟ وَتَوَاصَوْا۟ بِٱلصَّبْرِ وَتَوَاصَوْا۟ بِٱلْمَرْحَمَةِ

Identical actions reveal two reference points:

Action (Fi'l)	Direction (Wijha)	Reference/Intention
Freeing a slave	Compassion	Not political manipulation
Feeding an orphan	Divine Pleasure	Not social recognition

Outcome: True direction (tawjīh) transforms actors into: "Those who believe, urge one another to patience, and urge one another to compassion." → Ethical direction births moral community.

4. Qibla (قِبْلَة)
Beyond action (fi'l/فعل) and direction (wijha/وجهة), human endeavor requires an ultimate goal—the Qibla (قبلة) in Quranic terminology. This goal informs both right action and ethical

direction.

Through Ṣalah (prayer), Islam embedded the concept of Qibla into daily life. The Kaaba in Mecca—Allah's Sacred House (البيت الحرام)—serves as its tangible manifestation:

"The first House (of worship) established for mankind is the one at Bakkah (Mecca) – blessed and a guidance for all worlds." [3:96]

إِنَّ أَوَّلَ بَيْتٍ وُضِعَ لِلنَّاسِ لَلَّذِى بِبَكَّةَ مُبَارَكًا وَهُدًى لِّلْعَٰلَمِينَ

This unifying focal point continually reminds Muslims of their shared purpose. By introducing Qibla, Islam rendered abstract ideals like unity (waḥda/وحدة) concrete and accessible.

The Necessity of Ultimate Purpose:
Modern understanding affirms the critical role of societal qibla:
- It inspires collective movement toward transcendent objectives
- Mobilizes communities to overcome challenges
- Aligns individual actions with cosmic purpose

Islam presents Allah as the Ultimate Qibla, transcending all limitations:

"To Allah belong the East and the West. Wherever you turn, there is Allah's Presence." [2:115]

وَلِلَّهِ ٱلْمَشْرِقُ وَٱلْمَغْرِبُ ۚ فَأَيْنَمَا تُوَلُّواْ فَثَمَّ وَجْهُ ٱللَّهِ ۚ إِنَّ ٱللَّهَ وَٰسِعٌ عَلِيمٌ

"I have turned my face toward Him Who created the heavens and the earth – inclining toward truth, and I am not of those who associate others with Allah." [6:79]

إِنِّى وَجَّهْتُ وَجْهِىَ لِلَّذِى فَطَرَ ٱلسَّمَٰوَٰتِ وَٱلْأَرْضَ حَنِيفًا ۖ وَمَآ أَنَا۠ مِنَ ٱلْمُشْرِكِينَ

This Divine Qibla dissolves barriers of language, race, and status, unifying the Ummah around God as source of all high values:

"And He united their hearts. If you had spent all that is on earth, you could not have united their hearts, but Allah united them." [8:63]

وَأَلَّفَ بَيْنَ قُلُوبِهِمْ ۚ لَوْ أَنفَقْتَ مَا فِى ٱلْأَرْضِ جَمِيعًا مَّا أَلَّفْتَ بَيْنَ قُلُوبِهِمْ وَلَٰكِنَّ ٱللَّهَ أَلَّفَ بَيْنَهُمْ ۚ إِنَّهُ عَزِيزٌ حَكِيمٌ

"To Allah belong the East and the West; wherever you turn, there is Allah's countenance" [2:115]

Qibla as Long-Term Societal Catalyst Toward the Realization of Human as Divine Project
Islam established Qibla (قبلة) as the nucleus for civilizational vision. Hajj—a once-in-a-lifetime obligation—demands profound psychological and economic preparation. Historically, entire Muslim societies mobilized around this sacred journey:

"And proclaim to the people the Hajj; they will come to you on foot and on every lean camel, coming from every distant pass." [22:27]

وَأَذِّن فِى ٱلنَّاسِ بِٱلْحَجِّ يَأْتُوكَ رِجَالًا وَعَلَىٰ كُلِّ ضَامِرٍ يَأْتِينَ مِن كُلِّ فَجٍّ عَمِيقٍ

This collective endeavor manifested through:
- Architecture: Dedicated guest quarters (bayt al-ḍayf/بيت الضيف) in homes
- Community duty: Families providing lodging, sustenance, and moral support
- Tangible fulfillment: After lifelong prayer toward Qibla, pilgrims witness and touch it—proving transcendent goals are attainable through unity.

Qibla as Spatiotemporal Compass:
Ṣalah (prayer) transforms Qibla into existential orientation:
- Spatial awareness: Locating Qibla requires understanding one's earthly position (like a map's "You are here").
- Temporal rhythm: Fixed prayer times structure daily life:

"Prayer is enjoined upon the believers at prescribed times." [4:103]

إِنَّ ٱلصَّلَوٰةَ كَانَتْ عَلَى ٱلْمُؤْمِنِينَ كِتَٰبًا مَّوْقُوتًا

Direction vs. Goal: The Qibla Distinction:
Critical insight: While directions (wijah/وجهات) vary, the Qibla (goal) remains singular:
- Meccan model: Infinite radial paths converge at the Kaaba.
- Societal principle: Diverse methodologies across time/space are valid when aligned toward the same Qibla.

Ṭawāf (طواف): Unified Diversity in Motion:
Circumambulating the Kaaba embodies the Qibla as the harmonizing reference:
- Pilgrims traverse diverse stations (directions) while fixated on the singular Qibla.
- Symbolizes unity in purpose amid human plurality:

"Indeed, this community of yours is one community, and I am your Lord – so worship Me." [21:92]

إِنَّ هَٰذِهِ أُمَّتُكُمْ أُمَّةً وَٰحِدَةً وَأَنَا رَبُّكُمْ فَٱعْبُدُونِ

Qibla's Civilizing Reference:
Beyond ritual, the Qibla profoundly structured Muslim civilization by serving as the primary directional reference:
- Science: Astronomy and mathematics advanced expressly to determine global Qibla directions.
- Architecture: Homes faced the Qibla (not streets), as seen in rural

courtyards oriented toward Mecca.
- Ethics: Swearing oaths or slaughtering animals necessitated orientation toward Qibla—elevating mundane acts through transcendent intentionality.

The Imam embodies a realized closer state toward Qibla – a living reference demonstrating:
- Non-compulsive leadership:

"So remind, for you are only a reminder. You are not over them a controller." [88:21-22]

فَذَكِّرْ إِنَّمَا أَنتَ مُذَكِّرٌ (21) لَّسْتَ عَلَيْهِم بِمُصَيْطِرٍ

- Transparent accountability: Mistakes visibly corrected by congregation (contrasting hidden errors of followers).
- Organic succession: Leadership reflects spiritual maturity, per the Prophet's (ﷺ) directive:

"Let those of understanding and maturity stand closest to me." (Sahih al-Bukhari 735 -لِيَلِيَنِي مِنْكُمْ أُولُو الْأَحْلَامِ وَالنُّهَى), "Let those of understanding and maturity stand closest to me, then those next to them [in maturity]." Muslim 432 -لِيَلِيَنِي مِنْكُمْ أُولُو الْأَحْلَامِ وَالنُّهَى، ثُمَّ الَّذِينَ يَلُونَهُمْ)

The Ummah as Global Reference
The unified Qibla elevates Muslims to guide humanity as Allah's collective witness:

"Thus, We have made of you an Umma justly balanced, that you might be witnesses over the people and the Messenger a witness over you." [2:143]

وَكَذَٰلِكَ جَعَلْنَاكُمْ أُمَّةً وَسَطًا لِتَكُونُوا شُهَدَاءَ عَلَى ٱلنَّاسِ وَيَكُونَ ٱلرَّسُولُ عَلَيْكُمْ شَهِيدًا

This universal Umma-Imam manifests when:
- The societal Qibla anchors moral direction,
- Diversity harmonizes toward Divine purpose,
- Society becomes a reference of justice for all peoples.

Chapter Two

"Ayah": The Expression in The Cosmic Vision of Quran

Chapter Summary (Proposal)

This chapter explores the concept of "Ayah" (sign) as a central axis in the Quranic cosmic vision. It examines the linguistic, philosophical, and scriptural dimensions of "Ayah," showing how it connects Revelation, the Universe, and Human History. The chapter also clarifies the triadic framework of knowledge in the Quran and introduces the divine system of Creation and Command.

What is a Cosmic Vision?

A cosmic vision is a profound human understanding of how things in existence are ordered and interconnected. This vision is essentially an idea whose strength lies in its coherence and its capacity for interpretation.

"Ayah" as a Quranic Expression

The term "Ayah" (آية) is a uniquely Quranic concept and expression. It refers to anything that serves as a sign or milestone, pointing toward something beyond what is immediately visible.

"Do you build a landmark on every high place to amuse yourselves" [26:128]

أَتَبْنُونَ بِكُلِّ رِيعٍ آيَةً تَعْبَثُونَ

The word "Ayah" is also used to mean evidence or a sign pointing to an unseen truth.

"He said: O my Lord! Give me a sign" [19:10]

قَالَ رَبِّ اجْعَل لِّي آيَةً

Linguistically, "Ayah" is derived from the two Arabic letters: Alif (ألف) and Ya' (ياء), which together form "أي", an Arabic particle used to ask questions such as "who" or "which" in English. This suggests that the Quranic use of "Ayah" encourages readers to seek knowledge and approach the Truth through inquiry and questioning.

Contexts of "Ayah" in the Quran

The expression "Ayah" is used in the Quran within three primary contexts, as shown in Figure 1. Collectively, these contexts form the basis of what is proposed here as the cosmic vision of the Quran.

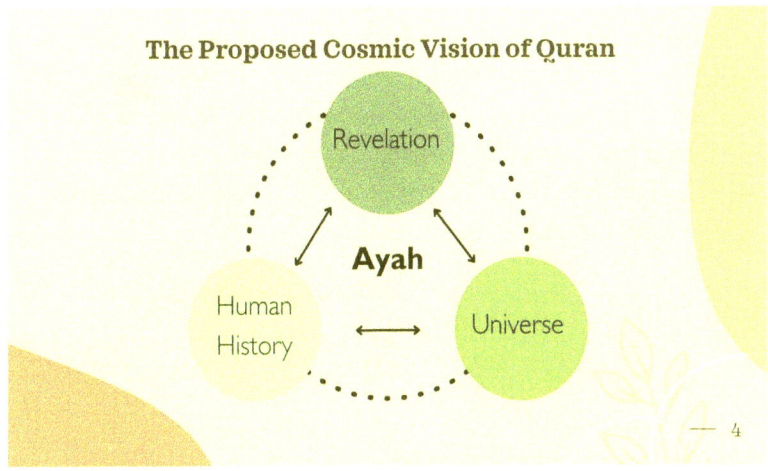

Figure 1. The Proposed Cosmic Vision of the Quran.

This diagram illustrates the integrative framework of the Quranic concept of "Ayah" (sign), which serves as the central axis connecting three fundamental domains: Revelation, Universe, and Human History. The figure depicts these domains as interconnected circles, each representing a distinct yet interrelated context in which "Ayah" operates. Arrows indicate the dynamic and reciprocal relationships among Revelation (divine communication), the Universe (the natural world), and Human History (the unfolding of human events). The dotted circular boundary emphasizes the holistic and interconnected nature of the Quranic worldview, wherein "Ayah" functions as a unifying principle that bridges scripture, creation, and historical experience.

"Ayah" in The Universe

The Quran uses the expression "Ayah" to describe various elements and phenomena in the universe.

"Behold! In the creation of the heavens and earth; in the alteration of the night and the day; in the sailing of the ships through the ocean for the benefit of mankind; in the rain which Allah sends down from the skies, and the life which he gives therewith to an earth that is dead; in the animals of all types that He scatters through the earth; and directing the wind; and the clouds which trail between the sky and the earth- indeed are signs for people who are wise" [2:164].

إِنَّ فِي خَلْقِ السَّمَاوَاتِ وَالْأَرْضِ وَاخْتِلَافِ اللَّيْلِ وَالنَّهَارِ وَالْفُلْكِ الَّتِي تَجْرِي فِي الْبَحْرِ بِمَا يَنفَعُ النَّاسَ وَمَا أَنزَلَ اللَّهُ مِنَ السَّمَاءِ مِن مَّاءٍ فَأَحْيَا بِهِ الْأَرْضَ بَعْدَ مَوْتِهَا وَبَثَّ فِيهَا مِن كُلِّ دَابَّةٍ وَتَصْرِيفِ الرِّيَاحِ وَالسَّحَابِ الْمُسَخَّرِ بَيْنَ السَّمَاءِ وَالْأَرْضِ لَآيَاتٍ لِّقَوْمٍ يَعْقِلُونَ

In this way, the Quran encourages its readers to look beyond natural causation and to see the elements and phenomena of the universe as signs pointing toward the unseen Truth—their Creator, who controls all things and is capable of changing them at any time (4)

"Say: see you? If Allah were to make the night perpetual over you to the Day of Judgment, what god is there other than Allah, who can give you enlightenment? Will you not then listen" [28: 71].

قُلْ أَرَأَيْتُمْ إِن جَعَلَ اللَّهُ عَلَيْكُمُ اللَّيْلَ سَرْمَدًا إِلَىٰ يَوْمِ الْقِيَامَةِ مَنْ إِلَٰهٌ غَيْرُ اللَّهِ يَأْتِيكُم بِضِيَاءٍ أَفَلَا تَسْمَعُونَ

Such change may appear as supernatural signs, or, in Quranic terminology, "greater signs" (آيات كبرى). These played a significant role in providing evidence for the authenticity of the Divine Message delivered by prophets before Prophet Muhammad (PBUH).

"That We may show you some of Our greater signs" [20:23]

لِنُرِيَكَ مِنْ آيَاتِنَا الْكُبْرَىٰ

During the Era of Prophet Muhammad (PBUH), people are directed to observe the universe around them to find these signs, rather than having their requests for supernatural signs fulfilled.

"They say: Why is not a sign sent down to him from his Lord? Say: Allah has certainly power to send down a sign: But most of them understand not. There is not an animal on the earth, nor a being that fly on its wings, but communities like you" [6:37-38]

وَقَالُوا لَوْلَا نُزِّلَ عَلَيْهِ آيَةٌ مِّن رَّبِّهِ قُلْ إِنَّ اللَّهَ قَادِرٌ عَلَىٰ أَن يُنَزِّلَ آيَةً وَلَٰكِنَّ أَكْثَرَهُمْ لَا يَعْلَمُونَ

وَمَا مِن دَابَّةٍ فِي الْأَرْضِ وَلَا طَائِرٍ يَطِيرُ بِجَنَاحَيْهِ إِلَّا أُمَمٌ أَمْثَالُكُم

"Ayah" in Quran

The Quran is divided into 114 chapters, each called a "Surah" (سورة)—a term unique to the Quran. Etymologically, "Surah" is related to "Soor" (سور), meaning a wall or a fence, suggesting a distinct structure or boundary. Each Surah is composed of verses known as "Ayat" (آيات), which serve as its fundamental building blocks. Every "Ayah" (آية), or verse, is a complete unit of meaning, often presenting a question or prompting reflection for the reader who seeks understanding (5).

"Ayah" in Human History

The Quran also uses the term "Ayah" to refer to the most significant historical accounts, narrated with accuracy and purpose. Readers are encouraged to extract lessons and morals from these stories:

"There was certainly in their stories a lesson for those of understanding" [12:111]

لَقَدْ كَانَ فِي قَصَصِهِمْ عِبْرَةٌ لِأُولِي الْأَلْبَابِ

These stories also serve as a powerful source of encouragement and reassurance:

"Each story We relate to you from the news of the messengers is that by which We make your heart firm" [11:120]

وَكُلًّا نَقُصُّ عَلَيْكَ مِنْ أَنبَاءِ الرُّسُلِ مَا نُثَبِّتُ بِهِ فُؤَادَكَ

By labeling these accounts as "Ayat," the Quran liberates its readers from being bound by immediate social laws, inviting them instead to perceive the Divine control behind these laws. Surah Al-Shu'araa provides an excellent example, where the following two verses are repeated after each historical narrative:

"Indeed, in that is a sign, but most of them were not believers. Indeed, your Lord is Ever Powerful, Ever Merciful" [26:67-68]

إِنَّ فِي ذَٰلِكَ لَآيَةً وَمَا كَانَ أَكْثَرُهُم مُّؤْمِنِينَ

وَإِنَّ رَبَّكَ لَهُوَ الْعَزِيزُ الرَّحِيمُ

The Triad: Universe, Revelation, and History

How do the Universe, Divine Revelation, and Human History interact to serve as sources of knowledge and guide the human experience? A continuous understanding of the Universe and the relationships among its elements and phenomena provides a reference point for human action. The Universe acts as a vast laboratory, validating whether human actions are possible and effective. For example, if an engineer constructs a building and it collapses, it is understood that the failure resulted from a miscalculation. On a deeper level, this means the action did not succeed because it was not in harmony with the laws governing the Universe. No one would claim the engineer was correct and the

Universe was at fault; rather, the situation must be reassessed, the question reformulated, and the approach adjusted. Thus, the Universe stands as the independent reference for human action (مرجع الفعل البشري).

When it comes to the meaning and direction of human action, the Universe does not intervene. Returning to the example of the building: if the construction is structurally sound and aligns with the laws of the Universe, the Universe does not determine how that building will be used. Will it serve a beneficial purpose or a harmful one? The answer to this question comes from a different reference point.

When the Quran describes itself as guidance for humanity—

"A guidance for the people..." [Quran 2:185]

هُدًى لِّلنَّاسِ

—it positions itself as the reference that provides human action with the direction of Truth and Goodness. In this sense, Revelation is the independent reference for direction (مرجع الوجهة).

All attempts to determine the direction of human action are never absolute; they must always remain open to adjustment in response to changes in time, place, and circumstance. While the words of the Quran are finite as "signifiers" (in their verbal expression), they are infinitely rich as "signifieds," offering limitless meanings and connotations.

"Say: If the ocean were ink to write the words of my Lord, sooner the ocean would be exhausted than the words of my Lord, even if we added another ocean like it for its aid" [18:109]

قُل لَّوْ كَانَ الْبَحْرُ مِدَادًا لِّكَلِمَاتِ رَبِّي لَنَفِدَ الْبَحْرُ قَبْلَ أَن تَنفَدَ كَلِمَاتُ رَبِّي وَلَوْ جِئْنَا بِمِثْلِهِ مَدَدًا

"If all the trees on earth were pens and the ocean with seven oceans behind it to add to its supply, yet the word of Allah would not be exhausted: For Allah is Exalted in power full of wisdom" [31:27]

وَلَوْ أَنَّمَا فِي الْأَرْضِ مِن شَجَرَةٍ أَقْلَامٌ وَالْبَحْرُ يَمُدُّهُ مِن بَعْدِهِ سَبْعَةُ أَبْحُرٍ مَّا نَفِدَتْ كَلِمَاتُ اللَّهِ إِنَّ اللَّهَ عَزِيزٌ حَكِيمٌ

In addition to the Universe as the reference for human action, and Divine Revelation as the reference for the direction of human action, human History serves as another essential source of knowledge. Once historical accounts are authenticated, they can be transformed into lessons and morals. In other words, human actions that have been validated by the Universe and whose direction aligns with Divine Revelation can be adopted and added to the collective human experience. Actions that are not validated by either or both references are to be rejected and avoided.

The three domains—the Universe, Divine Revelation, and human History—and their interrelations together constitute the cosmic vision of the Quran.

The Divine System of Creation and Command

Heaven, earth, and everything in between represent the cosmos, or the Universe, in Quranic terminology:

"We created the heavens and earth and all between them in six days" [50:38].

وَلَقَدْ خَلَقْنَا السَّمَاوَاتِ وَالْأَرْضَ وَمَا بَيْنَهُمَا فِي سِتَّةِ أَيَّامٍ

All of these are under the dominion of God:

"To Him belongs the dominion of heaven and earth" [57:2].

لَهُ مُلْكُ السَّمَاوَاتِ وَالْأَرْضِ

In Quranic terminology, dominion is called Mulk (ملك), while the command and governance of this dominion is referred to as Malakut (ملكوت):

"Thus We showed Abraham the realm and the command of the heavens and the earth." [Quran 6:75]

وَكَذَٰلِكَ نُرِي إِبْرَاهِيمَ مَلَكُوتَ السَّمَاوَاتِ وَالْأَرْضِ

"Do they not look into the realm of the heavens and the earth?" [Quran 7:185]

أَوَلَمْ يَنظُرُوا فِي مَلَكُوتِ السَّمَاوَاتِ وَالْأَرْضِ

In other words, both dominion (Mulk) and command (Malakut) belong to God alone:

"His is the creation and the command." [Quran 7:54]

أَلَا لَهُ الْخَلْقُ وَالْأَمْرُ

The triad of Revelation, the Universe, and human History all operate within the unified and integrated divine system of God's Creation and Command. In the next chapter, we will explore how the Beautiful Names of God and the high values derived from them form the conceptual and ethical framework of the Quran's cosmic vision.

Chapter Three

The Beautiful Names of God

A Conceptual and Ethical Framework

Chapter Summary (Proposal)
This chapter explores how the Beautiful Names of God provide the conceptual and ethical framework for the Quranic cosmic vision. It discusses the metaphysical nature of God, the significance of naming, the methodology of I'tibar, and the God-human relationship. The chapter also details how high values derived from the Divine Names guide human action and serve as universal standards for ethical conduct.

Human beings are reminded that their primary purpose in existence is to know God and draw closer to Him.

"But remind, for indeed the reminder benefits the believers. I have not created jinn and humankind except to worship Me." [Quran 51:55-56]

وَذَكِّرْ فَإِنَّ الذِّكْرَى تَنفَعُ الْمُؤْمِنِينَ

وَمَا خَلَقْتُ الْجِنَّ وَالْإِنسَ إِلَّا لِيَعْبُدُونِ

Knowing God Through His Beautiful Names

How do we come to know God? We do not know what God is in His essence. God is not part of the physical reality of the created universe; He is metaphysical. We cannot see God in this world:

"No vision can grasp Him, but His grasp is over all vision." [Quran 6:103]

لَا تُدْرِكُهُ الْأَبْصَارُ وَهُوَ يُدْرِكُ الْأَبْصَارَ

And there is nothing comparable to Him, so we cannot make an analogy or visualize Him:

"There is nothing whatever like unto Him." [Quran 42:11]

لَيْسَ كَمِثْلِهِ شَيْءٌ

However, we can learn who God is by understanding His attributes through His Beautiful Names. These names were the first knowledge imparted to Adam:

"And He taught Adam all the names." [Quran 2:31]

وَعَلَّمَ آدَمَ الْأَسْمَاءَ كُلَّهَا

The Power and Significance of Naming

What is the significance and power of a name? There are no thoughts or ideas without language. Language is the vehicle through which we express our thoughts. We assign names to things, ideas, and phenomena only after reaching a certain depth of understanding and forming concepts about them. Linguists have concluded that all human languages can be reduced to their basic units in the form of nouns, and "in reality, all things imaginable are but nouns." (6)

Commenting on the above Quranic verse, Iqbal said:

"Man is endowed with the faculty of naming things, that is to say, forming concepts of them, and forming concepts of them is capturing them. Thus, the character of man's knowledge is conceptual, and it is with the weapon of this conceptual knowledge that man approaches the observable aspect of Reality." (7)

This aligns with a major finding in recent cognitive science: "abstract concepts are largely metaphorical." (8)

In addition to being conceptual, human knowledge is also rational. The ability to name things enables us to distinguish and differentiate among them.

Naming the world is a dynamic process. Once something is named, the world itself can present new challenges, requiring us to develop new names and concepts. In this way, to name the world is to change it—human knowledge is therefore inherently transformative.

The Quranic verse mentioned above was revealed in response to the angels' questioning of humanity's legitimacy as stewards on earth:

"Behold, your Lord said to the angels: I will create a vicegerent on earth. They said: Will You place therein one who will make mischief and shed blood, while we celebrate Your praises and glorify Your holy name? He said: I know what you do not know." [Quran 2:30]

وَإِذْ قَالَ رَبُّكَ لِلْمَلَائِكَةِ إِنِّي جَاعِلٌ فِي الْأَرْضِ خَلِيفَةً قَالُوا أَتَجْعَلُ فِيهَا مَن يُفْسِدُ فِيهَا وَيَسْفِكُ الدِّمَاءَ وَنَحْنُ نُسَبِّحُ بِحَمْدِكَ وَنُقَدِّسُ لَكَ قَالَ إِنِّي أَعْلَمُ مَا لَا تَعْلَمُونَ

The ability to name things, ideas, and phenomena distinguished human beings from the very beginning—even from the angels—and represented a necessary, though not sufficient, condition for fulfilling their mission on earth.

The Concept of I'tibar in Approaching the Beautiful Names of God

Humans are continually invited to call upon God through His Beautiful Names and to draw closer to Him as devoted worshippers:

"The most beautiful names belong to Allah, so call on Him by them." [Quran 7:180]

وَلِلَّهِ الْأَسْمَاءُ الْحُسْنَىٰ فَادْعُوهُ بِهَا

At the same time, people are cautioned against following those who arrogantly deviate from the values derived from His Names:

"But shun those who profane His names; they will be requited for what they do." [Quran 7:180]

وَذَرُوا الَّذِينَ يُلْحِدُونَ فِي أَسْمَائِهِ سَيُجْزَوْنَ مَا كَانُوا يَعْمَلُونَ

Concepts such as justice, knowledge, mercy, forgiveness, and generosity are high values derived from the Beautiful Names of God: The All-Just, The All-Knowing, The Most Merciful, The All-Forgiving, and The Most Generous, respectively.

These high values must always guide the direction of human action. Realizing the Beautiful Names of God in human behavior thus becomes a divine experience. According to Ibn Arabi (9), this divine experience begins when a person feels the need to connect with the meaning or concept associated with one of God's Beautiful Names—a stage he called ta'alluq (تعلق). The second stage is tahaqquq (تحقق), when the individual internalizes and contemplates the Name, seeking to understand its meaning and how it can be actualized in practice. This leads to the final stage, takhalluq (تخلق), when the person embodies that Name and manifests it in their behavior and daily interactions.

In this way, humans acquire an empirical methodology to ensure their actions are rightly guided. This methodology is referred to as I'tibar (اعتبار).

It is noteworthy that the same term, I'tibar, was used for the concept of tajribah (تجربة), or laboratory experiment, in the works of the renowned physicist Ibn al-Haytham. He used it to demonstrate that the validity of human action is confirmed when it conforms to observable reality—that is, the physical universe (10). Ibn al-Haytham concluded that observable reality, verified through experimentation, must be the final arbiter among competing ideas about natural phenomena generated by speculative thinking. This marked a paradigm shift and the beginning of a new path: the scientific method.

The expression- I'tibar was also used by the celebrated historian, Ibn Khaldun to refer to the lessons or the morals generated from studying historical accounts (11). Ibn Khaldun gave his multi-volume book of history the title of "The Book of Al- Ibar" (كتاب العبر). Ibar and I'tibar are linguistically derived from Obour, عبور crossing i.e., moving from one side to another or moving from one human state to another. Conducting an experiment with verifiable results moves humanity into a new truth in the understanding of the Universe and its governing laws. Extracting the moral or the lesson from a historical account moves humans into a new state by heeding such lessons and avoiding previous mistakes. Practicing the high values derived from the Beautiful Names of God is the best way to move to a higher level of understanding these names and hence, know God better and get closer to Him.

God-Human Relationship
The Quran redefines the relationship between human beings and God. While God is the Highest (al-A'la, الأعلى), He is not distant or remote. Rather, He is intimately close to each person:

"We created man, and We know what his soul whispers to him; and We are closer to him than his jugular vein." [Quran 50:16]

وَلَقَدْ خَلَقْنَا الْإِنْسَانَ وَنَعْلَمُ مَا تُوَسْوِسُ بِهِ نَفْسُهُ وَنَحْنُ أَقْرَبُ إِلَيْهِ مِنْ حَبْلِ الْوَرِيدِ

God assures His worshippers of His nearness and responsiveness:

"When My servants ask you concerning Me, indeed I am near. I respond to the invocation of the supplicant when he calls upon Me. So let them respond to Me and believe in Me, that they may be rightly guided." [Quran 2:186]

وَإِذَا سَأَلَكَ عِبَادِي عَنِّي فَإِنِّي قَرِيبٌ أُجِيبُ دَعْوَةَ الدَّاعِ إِذَا دَعَانِ فَلْيَسْتَجِيبُوا لِي وَلْيُؤْمِنُوا بِي لَعَلَّهُمْ يَرْشُدُونَ

He is always present and ready to respond to His devoted worshippers, especially in times of necessity or distress:

"Or, who listens to the (soul) distressed when it calls on Him, and who relieves its suffering, and makes you (mankind) inheritors of the earth? Is there any god besides Allah? Little do you remember." [Quran 27:62]

أَمَّنْ يُجِيبُ الْمُضْطَرَّ إِذَا دَعَاهُ وَيَكْشِفُ السُّوءَ وَيَجْعَلُكُمْ خُلَفَاءَ الْأَرْضِ أَإِلَٰهٌ مَعَ اللَّهِ قَلِيلًا مَّا تَذَكَّرُونَ

Believers find satisfaction in God's response, which serves as the most practical and pragmatic evidence of His omnipresence (7).

In the Quran, humans are addressed as His devoted worshippers ('ibād, عباد), whom He cares for, sustains, and for whom He does not will injustice:

"Allah never wishes injustice to His creatures." [Quran 40:31]

إِنَّ اللَّهَ لَا يَظْلِمُ النَّاسَ شَيْئًا

"Allah means no injustice to any of His creatures." [Quran 3:108]

وَمَا اللَّهُ يُرِيدُ ظُلْمًا لِّلْعَالَمِينَ

Moreover, God is the One who initiates unconditional love towards His worshippers, even before they show love to Him:

"He loves them and they love Him." [Quran 5:54]

يُحِبُّهُمْ وَيُحِبُّونَهُ

He also expresses His pleasure with them before they are pleased with Him:

"Allah is well pleased with them, and they with Him." [Quran 98:8]

رَّضِيَ اللَّهُ عَنْهُمْ وَرَضُوا عَنْهُ

When humans diverge from this relationship, they remain 'ibād in the eyes of God, but they act as 'abīd (عبيد)—slaves to idols, masters, social status, desires, or even their own egos. In all Quranic verses where the word 'abīd is mentioned, it refers to those who have a negative relationship with God and are prisoners of their own false gods and wrongful actions:

"For Allah is never unjust to those who worship other gods." [Quran 8:51]

إِنَّ اللَّهَ لَيْسَ بِظَلَّامٍ لِّلْعَبِيدِ

Although linguistically 'ibād and 'abīd are both plurals of 'abd (عبد), they represent two contrasting paradigms and two diametrically opposed models of the human–deity relationship.

Based on this understanding, translating 'ibād Allāh (عباد الله) as "slaves of God" is inaccurate. Consequently, translating Islam as "submission" is also misleading. In fact, Islam is the peaceful acceptance of being among God's 'ibād. In this way, Islam as a state reflects the degree of freedom from anything that may come between humans and God. Such freedom allows humans to be elevated towards God, who is the Highest (al-Aʻla, الأعلى) and the Most Glorious (al-Majīd, المجيد), since nothing is above Him.

The Concept of Ibada

The concept of devoted worship ('ibādah) must be understood as knowing and drawing closer to God, as can be inferred from the following Quranic verses:

"But prostrate in adoration, and draw near [to Allah]." [Quran 96:19]

وَاسْجُدْ وَاقْتَرِبْ

"So fall down in prostration to Allah, and worship [Him]." [Quran 53:62]

فَاسْجُدُوا لِلَّهِ وَاعْبُدُوا

The essential question for humans, then, is: How should they move and elevate themselves towards God?

Humans move and elevate themselves towards God, their ultimate Qiblah, by embodying the high values derived from His Beautiful Names in both their private and social lives. Merely acknowledging that God is their Creator (Khāliq, خالق) and their Rabb (رب)—the One who brings creation to its perfection—is necessary but not sufficient. This acknowledgment is inherently performative; it calls for action and behavioral demonstration:

"Those who say, 'Our Lord is Allah,' and then remain steadfast…" [Quran 41:30]

إِنَّ الَّذِينَ قَالُوا رَبُّنَا اللَّهُ ثُمَّ اسْتَقَامُوا

The use of the particle thumma (ثُمَّ) in Arabic indicates that what follows is of a higher degree of significance, without diminishing the importance of what precedes it (3). Thus, realizing the high values and ethical ends derived from the Beautiful Names of God is the practical performance that gives substance to belief in God and His Names.

High Values Derived from the Beautiful Names of God

Four features characterize the high values derived from the Beautiful Names of God:

First, these values are universal. No individual or group has the right to monopolize them. When the Quran refers to high values or ethical ends, it does not qualify them as Islamic, Judeo-Christian, or Abrahamic; rather, they are described as maʿrūf (معروف), meaning universally known and evident:

"The believers, men and women, are protectors of one another. They enjoin what is right (maʿrūf) and forbid what is wrong…" [Quran 9:71]

وَالْمُؤْمِنُونَ وَالْمُؤْمِنَاتُ بَعْضُهُمْ أَوْلِيَاءُ بَعْضٍ يَأْمُرُونَ بِالْمَعْرُوفِ وَيَنْهَوْنَ عَنِ الْمُنكَرِ

Second, these high values are not only derived from the Beautiful Names of God but also have their reference and origin in Divine Revelation—the Quran. The Prophet Muhammad (peace be upon him) expressed this beautifully:

"Embrace the morals of God, and His morals are the Quran."

تَخَلَّقُوا بِأَخْلَاقِ اللَّهِ، وَأَخْلَاقُ اللَّهِ الْقُرْآنُ

The Prophet Muhammad was the first to embody these high values throughout his life. When his wife Aisha was asked about his moral conduct, she replied, "His moral conduct was the Quran."

كان خلقه القرآن

It is not by chance that many verses in the Quran conclude with certain Beautiful Names of God. These Names serve as important clues, guiding readers to interpret such verses in light of the values derived from them.

Third, while humans are free to choose any identities they wish, the Quran asserts that high values must take precedence over all other identities. Consider how the Quran introduces the values of truth and justice:

"O you who believe! Stand out firmly for justice, as witnesses to Allah, even if it be against yourselves, or your parents, or your kin, and whether it be (against) rich or poor: for Allah can best protect both. So follow not [personal] desires, lest you swerve, and if you distort [justice] or decline to do justice, verily Allah is well-acquainted with all that you do." [Quran 4:135]

يَا أَيُّهَا الَّذِينَ آمَنُوا كُونُوا قَوَّامِينَ بِالْقِسْطِ شُهَدَاءَ لِلَّهِ وَلَوْ عَلَىٰ أَنْفُسِكُمْ أَوِ الْوَالِدَيْنِ وَالْأَقْرَبِينَ إِنْ يَكُنْ غَنِيًّا أَوْ فَقِيرًا فَاللَّهُ أَوْلَىٰ بِهِمَا فَلَا تَتَّبِعُوا الْهَوَىٰ أَنْ تَعْدِلُوا وَإِنْ تَلْوُوا أَوْ تُعْرِضُوا فَإِنَّ اللَّهَ كَانَ بِمَا تَعْمَلُونَ خَبِيرًا

Here, the moral imperatives of truth and justice are placed above biology, social status, and all forms of expediency.

Fourth, the high values derived from the Beautiful Names of God serve as the standards by which humans judge and monitor the righteousness of their actions, thoughts, and feelings. For example, daily prayer is a divine experience, but its validity is confirmed only when it translates into practiced values such as care, generosity, and community service:

"Have you seen the one who denies the Judgment? Then such is the one who repulses the orphan and does not encourage the feeding of the poor. So woe to those who pray but are heedless of their prayer—those who make a show [of their deeds] and withhold [simple] assistance." [Quran 107:1–7]

أَرَأَيْتَ الَّذِي يُكَذِّبُ بِالدِّينِ فَذَلِكَ الَّذِي يَدُعُّ الْيَتِيمَ وَلَا يَحُضُّ عَلَىٰ طَعَامِ الْمِسْكِينِ فَوَيْلٌ لِلْمُصَلِّينَ الَّذِينَ هُمْ عَن صَلَاتِهِمْ سَاهُونَ الَّذِينَ هُمْ يُرَاءُونَ وَيَمْنَعُونَ الْمَاعُونَ

In conclusion, humans must orient their actions according to the high values common to all. If these values are derived from the Beautiful Names of God, then these Names must form the conceptual and ethical framework within which the Quran's cosmic vision—and its practical operation—are to be understood (see Figure 2).

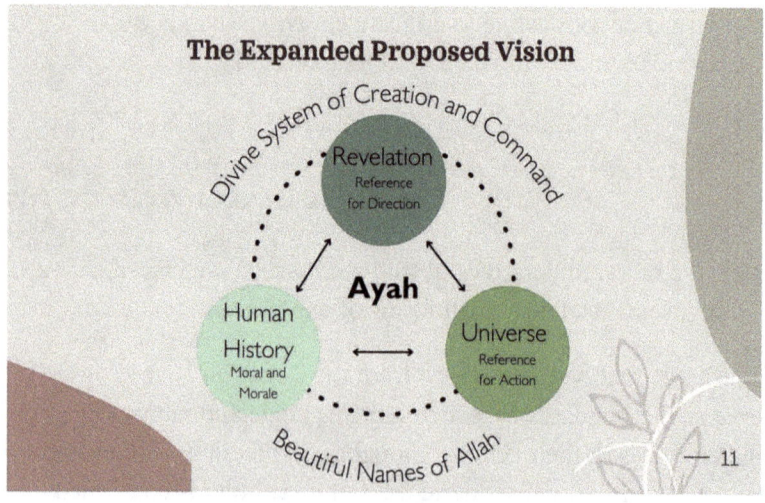

Figure 2: The Expanded Proposed Vision

This diagram illustrates the integrated framework of the Quranic worldview. At its center is the concept of "Ayah" (a sign or verse), surrounded by three interconnected domains: Revelation (reference for direction), Human History (moral and morale), and Universe (reference for action). These domains are dynamically linked, all operating within the Divine System of Creation and Command and reflecting the Beautiful Names of Allah. This vision emphasizes the harmonious relationship between revelation, human experience, and the universe, guiding ethical action and understanding in a diverse and interconnected world.

Chapter Four

The Universe in The Cosmic Vision of the Quran

Chapter Summary (Proposal)
This chapter explores the Quranic vision of the universe as conscious, sensitive, purposeful, and inherently diverse. It discusses the creation of the universe, its role as a reference for human action, the concept of tasbeeh (glorification), the relationship between humans and the universe, and the unique human project of self-definition and stewardship.

Creation of the Universe: Six Periods
The creation of the universe—comprising the heavens and the earth—was completed over six distinct periods or cycles of time. The Quran refers to these periods as "days" (أيام).

"Verily your Lord is Allah, Who created the heavens and the earth in six days." [10:3]

إِنَّ رَبَّكُمُ اللَّهُ الَّذِي خَلَقَ السَّمَاوَاتِ وَالْأَرْضَ فِي سِتَّةِ أَيَّامٍ

Of these six periods, the creation of the earth itself took two, establishing a ratio of 1:3.

"Say: Is it that you deny Him Who created the earth in two Days? And do you join equals with Him? He is the Lord of (all) the Worlds." [41:9]

قُلْ أَئِنَّكُمْ لَتَكْفُرُونَ بِالَّذِي خَلَقَ الْأَرْضَ فِي يَوْمَيْنِ وَتَجْعَلُونَ لَهُ أَندَادًا ۚ ذَٰلِكَ رَبُّ الْعَالَمِينَ

It is noteworthy that, according to the most recent scientific estimates, the ratio of the earth's age (4.543 billion years) to the age of the universe (13.7 billion years) is also approximately 1:3.

The Universe as the Reference for Human Action

The Universe satisfied two conditions in order to act as the reference of human action: Truth "See you not that Allah created the heavens and the earth in Truth?" [14:19] and balance "And the Firmament has He raised high, and He has set up the Balance" [55:7], "And the earth We have spread out; set thereon mountains firm and immovable; and produced therein all kinds of things in due balance" [15:19]. The fine tuning innately found in the physical Universe is also present in the Revelation "The Word of your Lord does find its fulfilment in truth and in justice" [6:115]. However, balance in the human realm or fine tuning is a challenge. Humans are in constant need for balance or fine tuning in order to resist extremes in both directions. Humans have the potential to go to one extreme by rejecting this world, turning their backs to it, and refusing to create and add into it. They can also go to the other extreme and transgress all boundaries, lose control, and lose their humanity.

How the Universe is Presented to Humans

The Universe in the cosmic vision of Quran is not inert or brute; but conscious, sensitive, and purposeful. The universe actively participates in glorifying its Creator, an act referred to in the Quran as "Tasbeeh" (تسبيح).

"The seven heavens and the earth, and all beings therein, declare His glory: there is not a thing but celebrates His praise; and yet you understand not how they declare His glory." [17:44]

تُسَبِّحُ لَهُ السَّمَاوَاتُ السَّبْعُ وَالْأَرْضُ وَمَنْ فِيهِنَّ وَإِن مِّن شَيْءٍ إِلَّا يُسَبِّحُ بِحَمْدِهِ وَلَٰكِن لَّا تَفْقَهُونَ تَسْبِيحَهُمْ

The universe operates under Divine command and control, functioning without error or deviation.

"It is not permitted to the Sun to catch up to the Moon, nor can the Night outstrip the Day: each swims along in its orbit." [36:40]

لَا الشَّمْسُ يَنْبَغِي لَهَا أَن تُدْرِكَ الْقَمَرَ وَلَا اللَّيْلُ سَابِقُ النَّهَارِ وَكُلٌّ فِي فَلَكٍ يَسْبَحُونَ

Tasbeeh (تسبيح) is a way to acknowledge that the Creator is beyond error or deficiency. For humans, who are always at risk of making mistakes, tasbeeh serves as a means to transcend error. The story of Prophet Jonah (Yunus) illustrates this: he turned to tasbeeh to free himself from the belly of the whale after being disciplined by God for abandoning his people.

"Had it not been that he glorified Allah, he would certainly have remained inside the Fish till the Day of Resurrection." [37:143-144]

فَلَوْلَا أَنَّهُ كَانَ مِنَ الْمُسَبِّحِينَ لَلَبِثَ فِي بَطْنِهِ إِلَىٰ يَوْمِ يُبْعَثُونَ

The various elements of the universe also engage in prostration, or "Sojoud" (سجود), to their Creator as a sign of their obedience and closeness to God.

"See you not to Allah bow down in worship all things that are in the heavens and on earth, the sun, the moon, the stars, the hills, the trees, the animals, and a great number among mankind." [22:18]

أَلَمْ تَرَ أَنَّ اللَّهَ يَسْجُدُ لَهُ مَن فِي السَّمَاوَاتِ وَمَن فِي الْأَرْضِ وَالشَّمْسُ وَالْقَمَرُ وَالنُّجُومُ وَالْجِبَالُ وَالشَّجَرُ وَالدَّوَابُّ وَكَثِيرٌ مِّنَ النَّاسِ

This verse distinguishes between humans and the rest of the universe regarding sojoud. For humans, prostration is a conscious act of will and choice, while for the rest of creation, it is instinctive and inherent.

The rest of the universe also acknowledges its obedience and loyalty to its Creator. The Quran refers to this as "Islam" (إسلام), meaning that all elements of creation turn only to God and always obey His commands.

"Moreover, He comprehended in His design the sky, and it had been (as) smoke: He said to it and to the earth: Come you together, willingly or unwillingly. They said: We do come in willing obedience." [41:11]

ثُمَّ اسْتَوَىٰ إِلَى السَّمَاءِ وَهِيَ دُخَانٌ فَقَالَ لَهَا وَلِلْأَرْضِ ائْتِيَا طَوْعًا أَوْ كَرْهًا قَالَتَا أَتَيْنَا طَائِعِينَ

In contrast, humans must make a conscious choice and liberate themselves from all attachments in order to turn to God in obedience.

"Say: We believe in Allah, and in what has been revealed to us and what was revealed to Abraham, Ismāʻīl, Isaac, Jacob, and the Tribes, and in (the Books) given to Moses, Jesus, and the prophets, from their Lord: we make no distinction between one and another among them, and to Allah do we admit (in Islam)." [3:84]

قُلْ آمَنَّا بِاللَّهِ وَمَا أُنزِلَ عَلَيْنَا وَمَا أُنزِلَ عَلَىٰ إِبْرَاهِيمَ وَإِسْمَاعِيلَ وَإِسْحَاقَ وَيَعْقُوبَ وَالْأَسْبَاطِ وَمَا أُوتِيَ مُوسَىٰ وَعِيسَىٰ وَالنَّبِيُّونَ مِن رَّبِّهِمْ لَا نُفَرِّقُ بَيْنَ أَحَدٍ مِّنْهُمْ وَنَحْنُ لَهُ مُسْلِمُونَ

When humans place their foreheads on the ground in prostration, they free themselves from their own ego—the strongest prison they must confront. In this act, the human is simultaneously the jail, the jailer, and the jailed. Prostration, for humans, is the ongoing ability to say "No" even to the highest level of spiritual attainment. In every unit of prayer, believers prostrate not once, but twice. Prostrating only once might give the false impression that the journey is complete. The Prophet Muhammad (PBUH) said: "The worshipper is closest to his Lord during prostration."

The Quran does not stop at the command to prostrate, but further instructs: "But bow down in prostration, and bring yourself the closer to Allah." [96:19]

وَاسْجُدْ وَاقْتَرِبْ

Thus, prostrating twice serves as a reminder of the long journey ahead and the need for continuous movement toward God—from the state of being to the state of becoming, and from clay to light. Rumi beautifully expressed this idea: "Go on a journey from self to self, my friend. Such a journey transforms earth into a mine of gold."

Like humans, the rest of the universe also receives Divine Commands in the form of Revelation, or "Wahy" (وحي). The various elements of the universe, whether vast like the heavens or the earth, or small like the bees, follow their respective revelations as direct commands to fulfill their assigned roles.

"So He completed them as seven firmaments in two Days, and He revealed to each heaven its duty and command." [41:12]

فَقَضَاهُنَّ سَبْعَ سَمَاوَاتٍ فِي يَوْمَيْنِ وَأَوْحَىٰ فِي كُلِّ سَمَاءٍ أَمْرَهَا

"When the Earth is shaken to her convulsion, and the Earth throws up her burdens, and man cries: What is the matter with her? On that Day will she declare her tidings: For that your Lord will have given her inspiration." [99:1-5]

إِذَا زُلْزِلَتِ الْأَرْضُ زِلْزَالَهَا وَأَخْرَجَتِ الْأَرْضُ أَثْقَالَهَا وَقَالَ الْإِنسَانُ مَا لَهَا يَوْمَئِذٍ تُحَدِّثُ أَخْبَارَهَا بِأَنَّ رَبَّكَ أَوْحَىٰ لَهَا

"And your Lord revealed to the Bee to build its cells in hills, on trees, and in human habitations." [16:68]

وَأَوْحَىٰ رَبُّكَ إِلَى النَّحْلِ أَنِ اتَّخِذِي مِنَ الْجِبَالِ بُيُوتًا وَمِنَ الشَّجَرِ وَمِمَّا يَعْرِشُونَ

Each of these creations follows its revelation as a direct command, fulfilling its unique role in the divine order.

By the time humanity entered the era of writing and reading, revelation to humans took the form of a "Divine Book" (كتاب إلهي). However, remaining committed to this revelation continues to be a challenge for humankind. There will always be those who follow it and others who refuse.

The rest of the universe is also sensitive; it does not welcome the sight of free-willed humans acting against the will of the Creator and disturbing the harmony of existence. The Quran describes how the heavens and the earth react when some people falsely claim that God has a child:

"They say: The Most Gracious has begotten a son! Indeed, you have put forth a thing most monstrous! At it the skies are ready to burst, the earth to split asunder, and the mountains to fall down in utter ruin, that they should invoke a son for Most Gracious. For it is not consonant with the majesty of the Most Gracious that He should beget a son." [19:88-92]

وَقَالُوا اتَّخَذَ الرَّحْمَٰنُ وَلَدًا ۞ لَقَدْ جِئْتُمْ شَيْئًا إِدًّا ۞ تَكَادُ السَّمَاوَاتُ يَتَفَطَّرْنَ مِنْهُ وَتَنشَقُّ الْأَرْضُ وَتَخِرُّ الْجِبَالُ هَدًّا ۞ أَن دَعَوْا لِلرَّحْمَٰنِ وَلَدًا ۞ وَمَا يَنبَغِي لِلرَّحْمَٰنِ أَن يَتَّخِذَ وَلَدًا

The universe is also purposeful; its creation is always linked to the goal assigned to it. Its form and purpose are always in harmony.

"He said: Our Lord is He Who gave to each thing its form and nature, and further, gave guidance." [20:50]

قَالَ رَبُّنَا الَّذِي أَعْطَىٰ كُلَّ شَيْءٍ خَلْقَهُ ثُمَّ هَدَىٰ

The Organic Relationship Between Humans and the Universe

Why is it important for humans to view the universe not as inert or brute? First, there is an organic relationship between humans and the rest of the universe. Both share the same origin: clay, with all its physical and chemical properties.

"From the (earth) did We create you, and into it shall We return you, and from it shall We bring you out once again." [20:55]

مِنْهَا خَلَقْنَاكُمْ وَفِيهَا نُعِيدُكُمْ وَمِنْهَا نُخْرِجُكُمْ تَارَةً أُخْرَىٰ

Therefore, humans and the universe are companions, not adversaries. However, humans are not meant to remain prisoners of the clay; they must transcend it in order to fulfill their unique role in existence.

Secondly, by recognizing that they are surrounded by conscious beings in their own unique ways, humans must not seek to "conquer" the rest of the universe, but rather to live peacefully in the earth, not merely on it. They are called to act as trustees or custodians, responsible for all the resources entrusted to them by their Creator.

"Behold, your Lord said to the angels: I will create a trustee in the earth." [2:30]

وَإِذْ قَالَ رَبُّكَ لِلْمَلَائِكَةِ إِنِّي جَاعِلٌ فِي الْأَرْضِ خَلِيفَةً

Humans are accountable for the resources provided to them and must not pollute the environment, abuse resources, or cause harm to any part of the universe in any form.

"It is He Who has created for you all things that are on earth; moreover, His design comprehended the heavens, for He gave order and perfection to the seven firmaments; and of all things He has perfect knowledge." [2:29]

هُوَ الَّذِي خَلَقَ لَكُم مَّا فِي الْأَرْضِ جَمِيعًا ثُمَّ اسْتَوَىٰ إِلَى السَّمَاءِ فَسَوَّاهُنَّ سَبْعَ سَمَاوَاتٍ وَهُوَ بِكُلِّ شَيْءٍ عَلِيمٌ

"When he turns his back, his aim everywhere is to spread mischief through the earth and destroy crops and cattle. But Allah loves not mischief." [2:205]

وَإِذَا تَوَلَّىٰ سَعَىٰ فِي الْأَرْضِ لِيُفْسِدَ فِيهَا وَيُهْلِكَ الْحَرْثَ وَالنَّسْلَ وَاللَّهُ لَا يُحِبُّ الْفَسَادَ

In this vision, humans are not owners, but stewards—entrusted with the care and preservation of the earth and all its resources, in harmony with the rest of creation.

Diversity in the Universe

In addition to being conscious, sensitive, and purposeful, the universe—including humanity—is inherently diverse.

"See you not that Allah sends down rain from the sky? With it We then bring out produce of various colors. And in the mountains are tracts white and red, of various shades of color, and black intense in hue. And so, amongst men and crawling creatures and cattle, are they of various colors. Those truly fear Allah, among His worshippers, who have knowledge: for Allah is Exalted in Might, Oft-Forgiving." [35:27-28]

أَلَمْ تَرَ أَنَّ اللَّهَ أَنزَلَ مِنَ السَّمَاءِ مَاءً فَأَخْرَجْنَا بِهِ ثَمَرَاتٍ مُخْتَلِفًا أَلْوَانُهَا وَمِنَ الْجِبَالِ جُدَدٌ بِيضٌ وَحُمْرٌ مُخْتَلِفٌ أَلْوَانُهَا وَغَرَابِيبُ سُودٌ *وَمِنَ النَّاسِ وَالدَّوَابِّ وَالْأَنْعَامِ مُخْتَلِفٌ أَلْوَانُهُ كَذَٰلِكَ إِنَّمَا يَخْشَى اللَّهَ مِنْ عِبَادِهِ الْعُلَمَاءُ إِنَّ اللَّهَ عَزِيزٌ غَفُورٌ

Humans are continually reminded of their diversity in gender, color, and language:

"And among His Signs is this, that He created for you mates from among yourselves, that you may dwell in tranquility with them, and He has put love and mercy between you: verily in that are Signs for those who reflect. And among His Signs is the creation of the heavens and the earth, and the variations in your languages and your colors: verily in that are Signs for those who know." [30:21-22]

وَمِنْ آيَاتِهِ أَنْ خَلَقَ لَكُم مِّنْ أَنفُسِكُمْ أَزْوَاجًا لِّتَسْكُنُوا إِلَيْهَا وَجَعَلَ بَيْنَكُم مَّوَدَّةً وَرَحْمَةً إِنَّ فِي ذَٰلِكَ لَآيَاتٍ لِّقَوْمٍ يَتَفَكَّرُونَ *وَمِنْ آيَاتِهِ خَلْقُ السَّمَاوَاتِ وَالْأَرْضِ وَاخْتِلَافُ أَلْسِنَتِكُمْ وَأَلْوَانِكُمْ إِنَّ فِي ذَٰلِكَ لَآيَاتٍ لِّلْعَالِمِينَ

Humanity is made up of different ethnic and racial groups. The purpose of this diversity is not conflict, but mutual learning, understanding, and cooperation. This process is called "ta'aruf" (تعارف) in the Quran:

"O mankind! We created you from a single pair of a male and a female, and made you into nations and tribes, that you may know each other." [49:13]

يَا أَيُّهَا النَّاسُ إِنَّا خَلَقْنَاكُم مِّن ذَكَرٍ وَأُنثَىٰ وَجَعَلْنَاكُمْ شُعُوبًا وَقَبَائِلَ لِتَعَارَفُوا

"Ta'aruf" goes beyond mere tolerance; it means valuing, respecting, and engaging with one another. Linguistically, "ta'aruf" is connected to "ma'ruf" (معروف), the universally recognized values shared by all humanity. People of diverse backgrounds are meant to cooperate in order to achieve "ma'ruf," which is the ultimate goal of "ta'aruf."

Creation in Pairs

Another universal phenomenon where humans and the rest of the Universe intersect is creation in pairs (الزوجية).

"And of everything We have created pairs: that you may bear in mind" [51:49].

This verse is followed by two verses; each one shows the implication of this phenomenon on the Creator and the created. The first, emphasizes the continuous reliance of the created on the Providence of the Creator "Hasten you then to Allah: I am from Him a Warner to you, clear and open" [51:50]. The second, acknowledges the unitary nature of God, the All-Rich (الغني), who is not in need of any partners or associates "And make no another an object of worship with Allah: I am from Him a Warner to you, clear and open" [51:51].

Definition: The Human Project

Humans differ from the rest of the Universe in the issue of definition. How do we define ourselves as human beings and who is responsible for this task?

In a Quranic Surah entitled "The Sun" ((الشمس) lies the answer as clear as the light of the sun. It starts by an oath:

"By the sun and its glorious splendor; by the moon as it follows; by the day as it shows up the sun's glory; by the night as it conceals it; by the heaven and its structure; by the earth and its expanse" [91:1-6]

As they are introduced in this oath; the sun, the moon, the day, the night, the heaven, and the earth are explicitly defined. They were given only one direction to follow since the time of their creation. None of them had or has the chance and the capability to change its mission, function, or course.

"It is not permitted to the sun to catch up with the moon, nor can the night outstrip the day: each swims along in its own orbit" [36:40]

"He said to heaven and to earth: come together willingly or unwillingly. They said: we do come in willing obedience" [41:11]

The Quranic discourse is a unique discourse, and the Arabic of Quran is a unique Arabic. Surah "Al-Shams" is a good demonstration of how the Quran utilizes the Arabic language and subjugates it to its cosmic outlook about Allah, the Universe, the Human being, and Life. The first six verses presented the different elements and phenomena of the Universe, each preceded by "the", the article that is used to point to a defined and specific object or an abstract idea. What about the human self or "nafs" that appeared in the seventh verse of the oath? Was it preceded or defined by the article 'the"? No!

"By every soul and the proportion and order given to it" [91:7]

In contrast with the Universe, each human soul is born without a predetermined definition. The task of defining the human soul is solely accomplished by itself and after it is borne into this life.

In contrast with the Universe that is unidirectional, human beings are given a dual or bidirectional nature: the ability to choose between two major directions:

"He enlightened it as to its wrong and its right" [91:8]

This freedom of choice grants all human beings the divine gift to define and add "the" to their souls.

Freedom of choice goes hand in hand with personal responsibility and accountability. The direction of "taqwa" leads to success; and wrongdoing leads to failure and disappointment.

"Truly he succeeds that purifies it, and he fails that corrupts it" [91:9]

In conclusion, humans have a unique place in this Universe. They are not better than any of its elements no matter how big or minute it may be. Although they have many things to share with the rest of the Universe, they have a different project. Part of this project is to preserve the well-being of the rest of the universe.

Chapter Five

The Name "Quran": A Novel Arabic Expression

Chapter Summary (Proposal)

This chapter explores the unique linguistic, structural, and functional features of the Quran as a novel Arabic expression. It discusses the types of expressions in the Quran, the etymology and structure of the term "Quran," and the dynamic processes of interpretation and application through tafseer and ta'weel.

Types of Expressions in Quran

There are three types of expressions, or "Mustalahat" (مصطلحات), found in the Quran:

a. Expressions Prevalent in Pre-Islamic Arabia:

Some expressions were already common in Arabia at the time of the Quran's revelation. The Quran adopted these as open linguistic containers, enriching them with new meanings and connotations. For example, the word "Salat" (prayer, صلاة) existed in Mecca before Islam, where it was practiced as whistling and clapping. The Quran refers to this:

"Their prayer at the House (of Allah) is nothing but whistling and clapping of hands." [8:35]

وَمَا كَانَ صَلَاتُهُمْ عِندَ الْبَيْتِ إِلَّا مُكَاءً وَتَصْدِيَةً

In Islam, prayer evolved into a comprehensive practice involving various states. Each state, such as bowing ("Ruku'", ركوع) or prostration ("Sujoud", سجود), has its own physical movement, each carrying unique moral and spiritual significance. For instance, "Tasbeeh" during "Ruku'" frees the believer from the prison of sin and error, while "Tasbeeh" during "Sujoud" liberates them from the prison of victory or high status, allowing them to draw closer to God. The Quran says:

"Nay, heed him not: but prostrate and bring yourself the closer (to Allah)." [96:19]

كَلَّا لَا تُطِعْهُ وَاسْجُدْ وَاقْتَرِبْ

b. Expressions for Pre-Existing Practices:

Some expressions describe concepts that were already practiced in daily life before being adopted by the Quran and becoming part of common language. A good example is "Ethar" (إيثار), which linguistically means favoring others in matters of personal need. The Quran describes this:

"And entertain no desire in their hearts for things given to others, but give them preference over themselves, even though poverty was their own lot." [59:9]

وَيُؤْثِرُونَ عَلَىٰ أَنفُسِهِمْ وَلَوْ كَانَ بِهِمْ خَصَاصَةٌ

If a culture does not practice "Ethar," it may not even have a word for it in its language.

c. Novel Quranic Expressions:

Some expressions are entirely new, representing unique Quranic terms or conventions. Examples include "Ayah" (آية) and "Surah" (سورة). The word "Quran" (قرآن) itself is a novel Arabic expression, used to describe the final Book of Revelation, and has become one of its names.

The Etymology of the Expression "Quran"

The term "Quran" first appeared in the history of revelation in Surah Al-Qiyama (The Resurrection, القيامة). From this, one can infer that the Quran was revealed to serve as a reference of meaning for humanity from the time of its revelation until the Day of Resurrection. Although the word "Quran" is a novel term, it is linguistically derived from well-known Arabic verbs: "Qara'" (قرأ), meaning "to read," and "Qarana" (قرن), meaning "to connect."

The Quran was revealed to Prophet Muhammad (PBUH) over a period of twenty-three years. Its verses, or "Ayat," were divinely connected and compiled into 114 chapters, known as "Surahs." The noble language, profound themes, and unique style and structure of the Quran set it apart from poetry and other forms of prose. As the Quran states:

"We have not instructed him (the Prophet) in Poetry, nor is it meet for him: this is no less than a Message and a Qur'ān making things clear." [36:69]

وَمَا عَلَّمْنَاهُ الشِّعْرَ وَمَا يَنبَغِي لَهُ ۚ إِنْ هُوَ إِلَّا ذِكْرٌ وَقُرْآنٌ مُّبِينٌ

In poetry, meanings and ideas are often shaped to fit the rhyme and meter. In contrast, in the Quran, any rhyme or rhythm serves the message and vision, not the other way around.

Structure and function of Quran

"Move not your tongue concerning the (Qur'ān) to make haste therewith. It is for Us to collect it and to construct it: But when We have constructed it, follow its structure. Nay more, it is for Us to explain it" [75:16-19]

لَا تُحَرِّكْ بِهِ لِسَانَكَ لِتَعْجَلَ بِهِ إِنَّ عَلَيْنَا جَمْعَهُ وَقُرْآنَهُ فَإِذَا قَرَأْنَاهُ فَاتَّبِعْ قُرْآنَهُ ثُمَّ إِنَّ عَلَيْنَا بَيَانَهُ

Verses 16–19 of Surah Al-Qiyama outline the structure and function of the Quran using expressions that reflect the original linguistic roots of this unique Arabic term:

a. Gathering and compiling the Quran into a single corpus ("jama'ahu" جمعه)

b. The style and structure of the Quran ("qur'anahu" قرآنه)

c. Clarifying the meaning of the Quran ("bayanahu" بيانه)

Groups of verses, ranging in size from 3 to 286, are compiled into Surahs. Al-Kawthar (الكوثر) is the shortest Surah, while Al-Baqara (البقرة) is the longest.

The divine compilation of the Quran resulted in perfect cohesion, or "Nazm" (نظم). This cohesion created a complete structure that allows for reading and multiple recitations—an "absolute reading." The Quran, in its entirety, is meticulously crafted and free from any distortion, described as "Muhkam" (محكم):

"Alif Lam Ra. This is a Book, with well-crafted verses, further explained in detail." [11:1]

الر تِلْكَ آيَاتُ الْكِتَابِ الْحَكِيمِ

Its various parts are also equal in their nobility and supreme style, known as "Mutashabih" (متشابه):

"Allah has revealed the most beautiful Message in the form of a Book, consistent with itself." [39:23]

اللَّهُ نَزَّلَ أَحْسَنَ الْحَدِيثِ كِتَابًا مُتَشَابِهًا

This perfect cohesion and the Quran's unique, readable structure not only contribute to its nobility but are also the source of its absolute clarity, or "Bayan" (بيان). This clarity is emphasized after the conjunctive particle "ثم" (then), which highlights the importance of what follows without diminishing what comes before.

The Expression of "Kalimat"

The Quran is composed of a finite number of words, or "Kalimat" (كلمات). As signifiers, these words have a limited range of pronunciations and tonalities. However, when approached as "signified," the words of the Quran possess limitless layers of meaning (12). The Quran illustrates this with the following verses:

"Say: If the ocean were ink to write out the words of my Lord, sooner would the ocean be exhausted than would the words of my Lord, even if we added another ocean like it, for its aid." [18:109]

قُل لَّوْ كَانَ الْبَحْرُ مِدَادًا لِّكَلِمَاتِ رَبِّي لَنَفِدَ الْبَحْرُ قَبْلَ أَن تَنفَدَ كَلِمَاتُ رَبِّي وَلَوْ جِئْنَا بِمِثْلِهِ مَدَدًا

"And if all the trees on earth were pens and the Ocean (were ink), with seven Oceans behind it to add to its (supply), yet would not the Words of Allah be exhausted: for Allah is Exalted in power, full of Wisdom." [31:27]

$$\text{وَلَوْ أَنَّمَا فِي الْأَرْضِ مِن شَجَرَةٍ أَقْلَامٌ وَالْبَحْرُ يَمُدُّهُ مِنْ بَعْدِهِ سَبْعَةُ أَبْحُرٍ مَّا نَفِدَتْ كَلِمَاتُ اللَّهِ إِنَّ اللَّهَ عَزِيزٌ حَكِيمٌ}$$

The Quranic term "Mathani" (مثاني), mentioned in the previously cited verse [39:23], is especially meaningful when considered alongside "Mutashabih." "Mathani" is the plural of "Thaniah," meaning "fold," while "Mutashabih" suggests that the words of the Quran remain fixed in form, but their meanings are dynamic and multi-layered.

The Expression "Umm Al-Kitab"

The revelation of the Quran occurred at the culmination of a long history of Divine Revelation. The Quran, along with the scriptures that preceded it, collectively belong to the "Mother of the Book," or "Umm Al-Kitab" (أم الكتاب):

"And verily, it is in the Mother of the Book, in Our Presence, high, full of wisdom." [43:4]

$$\text{وَإِنَّهُ فِي أُمِّ الْكِتَابِ لَدَيْنَا لَعَلِيٌّ حَكِيمٌ}$$

The evolution and progression of Divine Revelation over time reflect its primary purpose: to respond to the needs and challenges of humanity across different times and places.

The Expression of "Furqan"

Each Divine Book serves as a "Criterion," or "Furqan" (فرقان), for its era. This Quranic term highlights two important roles of Revelation. First, it describes the function of Revelation in distinguishing between truth and falsehood, or between good and evil. Second, it marks the transition between two distinct periods in human history, each with its own needs and challenges. With each new Revelation, the previous scripture is replaced as the Criterion for the new historical context.

"Tasdeeq" and "Hymana"

The process of replacement in Divine Revelation follows a clear approach based on two principles, each expressed by a distinct Quranic term:

• Endorsement ("Tasdeeq" تصديق): This principle involves reaffirming certain concepts that appeared in previous revelations.

• Overarching ("Hymana" هيمنة): This principle means that the new revelation overarches the previous one, providing humanity with new meanings and guidance suited to the challenges and questions of the new era.

For example, the Gospel of Jesus endorses the Torah of Moses and overarches it with new commandments:

"And to attest the Torah which was before me. And to make lawful to you part of what was forbidden to you." [3:50]

وَمُصَدِّقًا لِمَا بَيْنَ يَدَيَّ مِنَ التَّوْرَاةِ وَلِأُحِلَّ لَكُم بَعْضَ الَّذِي حُرِّمَ عَلَيْكُمْ

Similarly, the Quran endorses previous revelations and overarches them by addressing new challenges:

"To you We sent the Book in truth, confirming the Book that came before it, and overarching it." [5:48]

وَأَنزَلْنَا إِلَيْكَ الْكِتَابَ بِالْحَقِّ مُصَدِّقًا لِمَا بَيْنَ يَدَيْهِ مِنَ الْكِتَابِ وَمُهَيْمِنًا عَلَيْهِ

"Mutashabihat" and "Muhkamat"

The principles of endorsement ("Tasdeeq") and overarching ("Hymana") are closely related to two other Quranic expressions that categorize Quranic verses, from the perspective of the progression of Revelation, into two types:

- "Mutashabihat" (متشابهات): These are verses that endorse and echo verses from previous revelations. At first glance, they may appear repetitive or similar to earlier scripture. However, upon closer examination, they are restructured to fit the comprehensive framework and knowledge structure of the new Revelation.

- Muhkamat (محكمات): These are the original verses of the Quran that introduce new meanings and guidance for the final era of Prophet Muhammad (PBUH), which extends until the Day of Resurrection.

Both types of verses—Mutashabihat and Muhkamat—are mentioned in verse 7 of Surah Aal-Imran (آل عمران). Before this verse, the Quran describes the evolution of Revelation from the Torah to the Gospel to the Quran:

"It is He Who sent down to you the Book in truth, confirming what went before it; and He sent down the Torah and the Gospel before this, as a guide to mankind, and He sent down the criterion." [3:3-4]

نَزَّلَ عَلَيْكَ الْكِتَابَ بِالْحَقِّ مُصَدِّقًا لِّمَا بَيْنَ يَدَيْهِ وَأَنزَلَ التَّوْرَاةَ وَالْإِنجِيلَ مِن قَبْلُ هُدًى لِّلنَّاسِ وَأَنزَلَ الْفُرْقَانَ

There are some who do not recognize this evolution and wish for Revelation to remain fixed at the stage of the Torah or the Gospel. They focus only on the Quranic "Mutashabihat" verses, which resemble verses from the Torah or the Gospel, and therefore do not see the need for the Quran as a new Revelation. They overlook the "Muhkamat" verses of the Quran:

"It is He Who has sent down to you the Book; in it are original verses—they are the mother of the Book; others are similar to previous verses. But those in whose hearts is perversity follow the latter, seeking discord and searching for its final meaning, but no one knows its final meaning except Allah. And those who are firmly grounded in knowledge say: We believe in the Book; the whole of it is from our Lord. And none will grasp the message except people of understanding." [3:7]

هُوَ الَّذِي أَنزَلَ عَلَيْكَ الْكِتَابَ مِنْهُ آيَاتٌ مُحْكَمَاتٌ هُنَّ أُمُّ الْكِتَابِ وَأُخَرُ مُتَشَابِهَاتٌ فَأَمَّا الَّذِينَ فِي قُلُوبِهِمْ زَيْغٌ فَيَتَّبِعُونَ مَا تَشَابَهَ مِنْهُ ابْتِغَاءَ الْفِتْنَةِ وَابْتِغَاءَ تَأْوِيلِهِ وَمَا يَعْلَمُ تَأْوِيلَهُ إِلَّا اللَّهُ وَالرَّاسِخُونَ فِي الْعِلْمِ يَقُولُونَ آمَنَّا بِهِ كُلٌّ مِنْ عِندِ رَبِّنَا وَمَا يَذَّكَّرُ إِلَّا أُولُو الْأَلْبَابِ

"Tafseer" and "Taaweel"

Every reading of the Quran is an attempt to uncover or discover new meanings. This process is called "Tafseer" (تفسير), or interpretation—another Quranic expression, which appears only once in the Quran:

"And no question do they bring to you but We reveal to you the truth and the best explanation." [25:33]

وَلَا يَأْتُونَكَ بِمَثَلٍ إِلَّا جِئْنَاكَ بِالْحَقِّ وَأَحْسَنَ تَفْسِيرًا

Let us illustrate this process with two examples from Surah Al-Furqan, where this expression appears:

4. The Meccans questioned the human nature of the Prophet:

"And they say: What sort of a messenger is this, who eats food, and walks through the streets? Why has not an angel been sent down to him to give admonition with him?" [25:7]

وَقَالُوا مَالِ هَٰذَا الرَّسُولِ يَأْكُلُ الطَّعَامَ وَيَمْشِي فِي الْأَسْوَاقِ لَوْلَا أُنزِلَ إِلَيْهِ مَلَكٌ فَيَكُونَ مَعَهُ نَذِيرًا

The interpretation provided later in the same Surah is that the Prophet, like the messengers before him, is a teacher for humanity who shares their nature, understands their needs and feelings, and is familiar with their social circumstances:

"And the messengers whom We sent before you ate food and walked through the streets: We have made some of you as a trial for others: will you have patience? For Allah is One Who sees." [25:20]

وَمَا أَرْسَلْنَا قَبْلَكَ مِنَ الْمُرْسَلِينَ إِلَّا إِنَّهُمْ لَيَأْكُلُونَ الطَّعَامَ وَيَمْشُونَ فِي الْأَسْوَاقِ وَجَعَلْنَا بَعْضَكُمْ لِبَعْضٍ فِتْنَةً أَتَصْبِرُونَ وَكَانَ رَبُّكَ بَصِيرًا

b. The Meccans also questioned the manner in which the Quran was revealed, desiring it to be sent down all at once rather than gradually:

"Those who reject Faith say: Why is not the Qur'ān revealed to him all at once? Thus, We may strengthen your heart thereby, and We have rehearsed it to you in slow, well-arranged stages, gradually." [25:32]

وَقَالَ الَّذِينَ كَفَرُوا لَوْلَا نُزِّلَ عَلَيْهِ الْقُرْآنُ جُمْلَةً وَاحِدَةً كَذَلِكَ لِنُثَبِّتَ بِهِ فُؤَادَكَ وَرَتَّلْنَاهُ تَرْتِيلًا

The Quran itself provides the interpretation: its chapters and passages were revealed gradually in response to the circumstances and challenges faced by the Prophet and his community. This gradual revelation strengthened the faith of the Prophet and his companions, allowing the Quran to address new events and resolve confusion as they arose. Despite being revealed at different times and places, the Quran was ultimately compiled into coherent chapters, or Surahs.

Who needs interpretation—the Quran or us? It is not the Quran that needs interpretation; rather, we need the Quran to interpret us—our concerns, our challenges, and our affairs. We need the guidance and light of the Quran as we move forward in life.

This brings us to another process of interpreting the Quran: "Ta'weel" (تأويل). This expression appears fifteen times in the Quran and carries the connotation of predicting the future and determining the ultimate outcome or destination of different matters.

Relating Tafseer and Ta'weel: A Higher Level of Understanding

How can we use our imagination to connect the processes of Tafseer and Ta'weel at a deeper level? It is often said that life is understood backward but must be lived forward. In this sense, Tafseer is the intellectual effort to explain and interpret what has happened in the past, while Ta'weel is the forward-looking mental struggle—one that must be exerted even more—to derive new concepts, meanings, and applications that can improve our future.

Every era in human history has its own structure of knowledge and its own methodology for acquiring and organizing that knowledge. This field of study is known as epistemology. The Quran refers to its own epistemological methodology as "Minhaj" (منهاج), which must always accompany the Sharia (شريعة):

"To each among you have We prescribed a Law and a methodology." [5:48]

لِكُلٍّ جَعَلْنَا مِنكُمْ شِرْعَةً وَمِنْهَاجًا

Consider this example: The Quran poses a rhetorical question to people who are weak and oppressed, yet have resigned themselves to exploitation and subjugation:

"Wasn't God's earth spacious enough for you to migrate elsewhere and escape your persecution?" [4:97]

أَلَمْ تَكُنْ أَرْضُ اللَّهِ وَاسِعَةً فَتُهَاجِرُوا فِيهَا

Through Tafseer, this verse can be interpreted in light of the cultural and sociopolitical conditions at the time of the Quran's revelation—when there were no clear borders, passports, or emigration laws. However, within the epistemological paradigms of our age, and through the process of Ta'weel, the "space of earth" that needs to be reclaimed by the oppressed may not be geographical, but rather spiritual, moral, or intellectual. In this way, one can resist oppression and maintain autonomy of conscience even when physical migration, autonomy, and communal self-determination have become more challenging in the era of powerful nation-states, monitored borders, and strict immigration laws.

Therefore, the conclusions and recommendations made by scholars and experts today may differ from those intended in the original context, as they must respond to new realities and challenges.

The Quran is deeply concerned with preserving the ongoing movement of revelation through time. It warns against any attempt to bring revelation to a halt under any circumstances. Ta'weel must remain a continuous process, and only God knows the ultimate destination of revelation:

"But no one knows its final meaning except Allah." [3:7]

وَمَا يَعْلَمُ تَأْوِيلَهُ إِلَّا اللَّهُ

The Quranic expressions discussed above help us reconstruct a deeper understanding of the structure and function of the final Book of Revelation. The Quran is the culmination of the movement and evolution of revelation, preserved in the "Mother of the Book" (Umm Al-Kitab). The Quran retained parts of previous revelations as "Ayat Mutashabihat" because of their continued relevance, through the process of "tasdeeq" (endorsement). The rest were abrogated because they had become irrelevant in the new historical context. In other words, abrogation occurred in the Mother of the Book, not within the Quran itself:

"Allah does blot out or confirm what He pleases: with Him is the Mother of the Book." [13:39]

يَمْحُو اللَّهُ مَا يَشَاءُ وَيُثْبِتُ وَعِندَهُ أُمُّ الْكِتَابِ

The abrogated parts were replaced by new and original "Ayat Muhkamat":

"None of Our revelations do We abrogate or cause to be forgotten, but We substitute something better or similar." [2:106]

مَا نَنسَخْ مِنْ آيَةٍ أَوْ نُنسِهَا نَأْتِ بِخَيْرٍ مِنْهَا أَوْ مِثْلِهَا

This process of "hymanah" (overarching) [5:48] brings the final Revelation to a higher level of understanding, ensuring its relevance and guidance for every era.

"Tafseer" is the tool by which the "Ayat Mutashabihat" are understood within the new structure of knowledge provided by the Quran and its historical context. In this way, one could suggest that these verses are transformed into "Ayat Muhkamat." Surah Hud recounts the experiences of prophets who came before Prophet Muhammad (PBUH). These stories remain relevant, forming a unified and comprehensive guidance for humanity, as if they are unfolding in the present. It is noteworthy that Surah Hud begins by stating that all the verses of the Quran are made "Muhkamat" before being explained in detail:

"Alif Lam Ra. This is a Book, with well-crafted verses, further explained in detail." [11:1]

الر تِلْكَ آيَاتُ الْكِتَابِ الْحَكِيمِ

All the verses of the Quran were divinely compiled into well-structured constructs. The words of God are constant, but their meanings are continuously evolving through the process of "ta'weel."

"Ta'weel" can be defined as transforming the text into application. The major signs (miracles) performed by previous prophets were effective in confirming the truth of their message, but their impact diminishes as we move further away from them in time and space. In contrast, the signs of the final text—the Quran—remain open to interpretation through "ta'weel," and our understanding deepens as human knowledge and experience grow over time. The words of God are wholesome, like a fruitful tree that continually produces its fruit:

"Do you not see how Allah sets forth a parable? A good word is like a good tree, whose root is firmly fixed, and its branches reach to the heavens. It brings forth its fruit at all times, by the leave of its Lord." [14:24-25]

أَلَمْ تَرَ كَيْفَ ضَرَبَ اللَّهُ مَثَلًا كَلِمَةً طَيِّبَةً كَشَجَرَةٍ طَيِّبَةٍ أَصْلُهَا ثَابِتٌ وَفَرْعُهَا فِي السَّمَاءِ تُؤْتِي أُكُلَهَا كُلَّ حِينٍ بِإِذْنِ رَبِّهَا

Chapter Six

The Human in The Cosmic Vision of Quran

Chapter Summary (Proposal)

This chapter explores the Quranic vision of the human being, examining the various names and expressions used to describe humanity, the dual nature of human existence, and the unique role of humans as trustees and worshippers. It analyzes the stages of human movement and direction through key Quranic passages, highlighting the balance between action, guidance, and responsibility.

Names and Expressions for Human Beings

The Quran uses various names and expressions to refer to human beings, each highlighting a different aspect of human nature and function:

1. *Bashar* (بشر)

This term highlights the shared, complex makeup of all human beings: the physical body and the Divine spark, or "Rouh" (روح).

"Behold, your Lord said to the angels: I am about to create man from clay: When I have fashioned him and breathed into him of My spirit, prostrate down in obeisance unto him." [38:71-72]

إِذْ قَالَ رَبُّكَ لِلْمَلَائِكَةِ إِنِّي خَالِقٌ بَشَرًا مِّن طِينٍ فَإِذَا سَوَّيْتُهُ وَنَفَخْتُ فِيهِ مِن رُّوحِي فَقَعُوا لَهُ سَاجِدِينَ

"They ask you concerning the Spirit. Say: The Spirit comes by command of my Lord: of knowledge it is only a little that is communicated to you." [17:85]

وَيَسْأَلُونَكَ عَنِ الرُّوحِ قُلِ الرُّوحُ مِنْ أَمْرِ رَبِّي وَمَا أُوتِيتُم مِّنَ الْعِلْمِ إِلَّا قَلِيلًا

All "Bashar" are mortal:

"We granted not to any man before you a permanent life: if then you should die, would they live permanently? Every soul shall have a taste of death: and We test you by evil and by good by way of trial. To Us must you return." [21:34-35]

وَمَا جَعَلْنَا لِبَشَرٍ مِّن قَبْلِكَ الْخُلْدَ أَفَإِن مِّتَّ فَهُمُ الْخَالِدُونَ كُلُّ نَفْسٍ ذَائِقَةُ الْمَوْتِ وَنَبْلُوكُم بِالشَّرِّ وَالْخَيْرِ فِتْنَةً وَإِلَيْنَا تُرْجَعُونَ

Prophet Muhammad (PBUH) also emphasized his humanity, with the only distinction being that he receives Divine Revelation:

"Say: I am but a man like yourselves, but the inspiration has come to me." [18:110]

قُلْ إِنَّمَا أَنَا بَشَرٌ مِّثْلُكُمْ يُوحَىٰ إِلَيَّ

Even the Archangel Gabriel appeared to Mary (PBUH), the mother of Jesus (PBUH), in a form very close to a human "Bashar" at the time of the annunciation:

"She placed a screen from them; then We sent to her Our angel, and he appeared before her as a man in all respects." [19:17]

فَاتَّخَذَتْ مِن دُونِهِمْ حِجَابًا فَأَرْسَلْنَا إِلَيْهَا رُوحَنَا فَتَمَثَّلَ لَهَا بَشَرًا سَوِيًّا

2. Insan (إنسان)

This unique term denotes two human entities addressed as one, applying equally to both male and female human beings. It also reflects the dual nature of human tendencies toward both goodness and wickedness.

"Does man think that he will be left without a purpose? Was he not a drop of sperm emitted? Then did he become a leech-like clot; then did (Allah) make and fashion (him) in due proportion. And of him He made two sexes, male and female." [75:36-39]

أَيَحْسَبُ الْإِنسَانُ أَن يُتْرَكَ سُدًى أَلَمْ يَكُ نُطْفَةً مِّن مَّنِيٍّ يُمْنَىٰ ثُمَّ كَانَ عَلَقَةً فَخَلَقَ فَسَوَّىٰ فَجَعَلَ مِنْهُ الزَّوْجَيْنِ الذَّكَرَ وَالْأُنثَىٰ

The creation of "Insan" as a physical being began with clay:

"He Who has made everything which He has created best: He began the creation of man with clay." [32:7]

الَّذِي أَحْسَنَ كُلَّ شَيْءٍ خَلَقَهُ وَبَدَأَ خَلْقَ الْإِنسَانِ مِن طِينٍ

"Man We did create from a quintessence of clay." [23:12]

وَلَقَدْ خَلَقْنَا الْإِنسَانَ مِن سُلَالَةٍ مِّن طِينٍ

The duality embedded in the term "Insan" extends beyond gender, reflecting both good and evil tendencies, and the duality of action and direction.

"And its enlightenment as to its wrong and its right." [91:8]

فَأَلْهَمَهَا فُجُورَهَا وَتَقْوَاهَا

"And shown him the two highways." [90:10]

وَهَدَيْنَاهُ النَّجْدَيْنِ

Among all creations, "Insan" possesses the highest level of consciousness, including introspection:

"Nay, man has insight into himself." [75:14]

بَلِ الْإِنسَانُ عَلَىٰ نَفْسِهِ بَصِيرَةٌ

All human beings share the same "Fitra" (فطرة), the primordial human nature:

"So set you your face steadily and truly to the Faith: (establish) Allah's handiwork according to the pattern on which He has made mankind: no change in the work of Allah: that is the standard Religion: but most among mankind understand not." [30:30]

فَأَقِمْ وَجْهَكَ لِلدِّينِ حَنِيفًا فِطْرَتَ اللَّهِ الَّتِي فَطَرَ النَّاسَ عَلَيْهَا لَا تَبْدِيلَ لِخَلْقِ اللَّهِ ذَٰلِكَ الدِّينُ الْقَيِّمُ وَلَٰكِنَّ أَكْثَرَ النَّاسِ لَا يَعْلَمُونَ

"Fitra" is the Divine design that existed before time itself, preceding the creation of the heavens and the earth:

"Praise be to Allah, Who created according to His design the heavens and the earth." [35:1]

الْحَمْدُ لِلَّهِ فَاطِرِ السَّمَاوَاتِ وَالْأَرْضِ

3. Khalifa (خليفة): *Custodian or Trustee*

"Khalifa" represents the highest function of the human being on earth—a custodian or trustee.

"Behold, your Lord said to the angels: I will create a trustee in the earth." [2:30]

وَإِذْ قَالَ رَبُّكَ لِلْمَلَائِكَةِ إِنِّي جَاعِلٌ فِي الْأَرْضِ خَلِيفَةً

Humans are entrusted with the Divine spark and the high values embedded in "Fitra." They are the rightful trustees of all resources in the heavens and the earth:

"It is He Who has created for you all things that are on earth; moreover His design comprehended the heavens, for He gave order and perfection to the seven firmaments; and of all things He has perfect knowledge." [2:29]

هُوَ الَّذِي خَلَقَ لَكُم مَّا فِي الْأَرْضِ جَمِيعًا ثُمَّ اسْتَوَىٰ إِلَى السَّمَاءِ فَسَوَّاهُنَّ سَبْعَ سَمَاوَاتٍ وَهُوَ بِكُلِّ شَيْءٍ عَلِيمٌ

This responsibility is balanced by the high values derived from the Beautiful Names of God, taught to humanity through Adam:

"And He taught Adam all the names." [2:31]

وَعَلَّمَ آدَمَ الْأَسْمَاءَ كُلَّهَا

The "Trust" (أمانة) is immense, and the human being accepted it while the heavens, the earth, and the mountains refused:

"We did indeed offer the Trust to the Heavens and the Earth and the Mountains; but they refused to undertake it, being afraid thereof: but man undertook it." [33:72]

إِنَّا عَرَضْنَا الْأَمَانَةَ عَلَى السَّمَاوَاتِ وَالْأَرْضِ وَالْجِبَالِ فَأَبَيْنَ أَن يَحْمِلْنَهَا وَأَشْفَقْنَ مِنْهَا وَحَمَلَهَا الْإِنسَانُ

The Quran consistently describes the "Khalifa" as being "in" the earth, not just "on" it:

"He it is that has made you trustees in the earth." [35:39]

هُوَ الَّذِي جَعَلَكُمْ خَلَائِفَ فِي الْأَرْضِ

And to build "in" the earth, not just "on" it:

"It is He Who has produced you from the earth and settled you therein." [11:61]

هُوَ أَنشَأَكُم مِّنَ الْأَرْضِ وَاسْتَعْمَرَكُمْ فِيهَا

As custodians, humans are responsible for protecting the resources of the heavens and the earth from misuse, abuse, or exploitation. To fulfill this trust, humans must be aware of the diseases and barriers that prevent them from carrying out their responsibility. These include injustice and ignorance (disregarding ethics):

"Man was indeed unjust and ignorant." [33:72]

إِنَّهُ كَانَ ظَلُومًا جَهُولًا

Other obstacles include ingratitude, denial of the truth, weakness, misery, endless arguing, hastiness, and total loss.

4. Ibadullah (عباد الله) – *Worshippers of God*

In the Quran, humans are addressed as devoted worshippers, "Ibad" (عباد), whom God cares for and sustains:

"Allah never wishes injustice to His worshippers." [40:31]

وَمَا اللَّهُ يُرِيدُ ظُلْمًا لِلْعِبَادِ

"These are the Signs of Allah: We rehearse them to you in Truth: and Allah means no injustice to any of His creatures." [3:108]

تِلْكَ آيَاتُ اللَّهِ نَتْلُوهَا عَلَيْكَ بِالْحَقِّ وَمَا اللَّهُ يُرِيدُ ظُلْمًا لِلْعَالَمِينَ

This address represents the highest purpose of human creation:

"I have only created Jinns and men, that they may worship Me." [51:56]

وَمَا خَلَقْتُ الْجِنَّ وَالْإِنسَ إِلَّا لِيَعْبُدُونِ

Believers express their commitment to this purpose in their daily recitation of Surah Al-Fatiha:

"In the name of Allah, Most Gracious, Most Merciful. Praise be to Allah, the Cherisher and Sustainer of the Worlds; Most Gracious, Most Merciful; Master of the Day of Judgement. You do we worship, and Your aid we seek." [1:1–5]

بِسْمِ اللَّهِ الرَّحْمَٰنِ الرَّحِيمِ الْحَمْدُ لِلَّهِ رَبِّ الْعَالَمِينَ الرَّحْمَٰنِ الرَّحِيمِ مَالِكِ يَوْمِ الدِّينِ إِيَّاكَ نَعْبُدُ وَإِيَّاكَ نَسْتَعِينُ

Stages of the Human Journey in the Quranic Vision

The early, concise passages of the Quran outline the stages of the shared human journey. The following four constructs illustrate the main stages of this enterprise:

5. Surah Al-'Alaq

The first stage involves two types of reading:

4. Reading to create: "Read in the name of your Lord, Who created; Created man, out of a clot of blood." [96:1-2]

اقْرَأْ بِاسْمِ رَبِّكَ الَّذِي خَلَقَ خَلَقَ الْإِنسَانَ مِنْ عَلَقٍ

b. Reading to learn: "Read! And your Lord is Most Bountiful, He Who taught by the Pen, taught man that which he knew not." [96:3-5]

اقْرَأْ وَرَبُّكَ الْأَكْرَمُ الَّذِي عَلَّمَ بِالْقَلَمِ عَلَّمَ الْإِنسَانَ مَا لَمْ يَعْلَمْ

As a warning, the Prophet (PBUH) is called to rise and deliver a message: "O you wrapped up! Arise and deliver your warning." [74:1-2]

يَا أَيُّهَا الْمُدَّثِّرُ قُمْ فَأَنذِرْ

The Prophet's warning is first and foremost against self-sufficiency, which leads to transgression and imbalance: "Nay, but man does transgress all bounds, in that he looks upon himself as self-sufficient." [96:6-7]

كَلَّا إِنَّ الْإِنسَانَ لَيَطْغَىٰ أَن رَّآهُ اسْتَغْنَىٰ

Human beings are in dire need of balance in their lives to protect themselves from transgression. This balance is like the fine-tuning seen in the Universe: "And the sky He has raised high, and He has set up the balance, in order that you may not transgress (due) balance. So establish weight with justice and fall not short in the balance." [55:7-9]

وَالسَّمَاءَ رَفَعَهَا وَوَضَعَ الْمِيزَانَ أَلَّا تَطْغَوْا فِي الْمِيزَانِ وَأَقِيمُوا الْوَزْنَ بِالْقِسْطِ وَلَا تُخْسِرُوا الْمِيزَانَ

And in the Revelation: "The word of your Lord has been fulfilled in truth and in justice." [6:115]

وَتَمَّتْ كَلِمَتُ رَبِّكَ صِدْقًا وَعَدْلًا

6. Surah Al-layl

This Surah elaborates on the wide range of human behavior and movement: "By the creation of male and female; Verily, your strife is diverse. So, he who gives and fears (Allah), and testifies to the best, We will indeed make smooth for him the path to Bliss. But he who is a greedy miser and thinks himself self-sufficient, and gives the lie to the Best, We will indeed make smooth for him the path to Misery." [92:3-10]

وَمَا خَلَقَ الذَّكَرَ وَالْأُنْثَىٰ إِنَّ سَعْيَكُمْ لَشَتَّىٰ فَأَمَّا مَنْ أَعْطَىٰ وَاتَّقَىٰ وَصَدَّقَ بِالْحُسْنَىٰ فَسَنُيَسِّرُهُ لِلْيُسْرَىٰ وَأَمَّا مَن بَخِلَ وَاسْتَغْنَىٰ وَكَذَّبَ بِالْحُسْنَىٰ فَسَنُيَسِّرُهُ لِلْعُسْرَىٰ

7. Surah Al-Shams

Surah Al-Shams centers on the challenge of the direction of human movement: "By the Soul, and the proportion and order given to it; and its enlightenment as to its wrong and its right." [91:7-8]

وَنَفْسٍ وَمَا سَوَّاهَا فَأَلْهَمَهَا فُجُورَهَا وَتَقْوَاهَا

Unlike the rest of creation, the human being is not born with a predetermined direction. Each person must define their own path, and the outcome depends on the choices they make: "Truly he succeeds that purifies it, and he fails that corrupts it." [91:9-10]

قَدْ أَفْلَحَ مَن زَكَّاهَا وَقَدْ خَابَ مَن دَسَّاهَا

8. Surah Al-Duha

Surah Al-Duha highlights the importance of Revelation in providing guidance for the direction of human movement. "Al-Duha" (الضحى) refers to the forenoon or the youth of the day, serving as a metaphor for the light and vitality brought by Revelation: "By the Glorious Morning Light." [93:1]

وَالضُّحَىٰ

The absence of Revelation in human life is likened to death and the darkness of night: "And by the Night when it is still." [93:2]

وَاللَّيْلِ إِذَا سَجَىٰ

God's commitment to humanity is clear—He will not leave people without guidance: "Your Guardian-Lord has not forsaken you, nor is He displeased." [93:3]

مَا وَدَّعَكَ رَبُّكَ وَمَا قَلَىٰ

And what is to come will be even better: "And verily the Hereafter will be better for you than the present. And soon will your Guardian-Lord give you what you shall be well-pleased." [93:4-5]

وَلَلْآخِرَةُ خَيْرٌ لَّكَ مِنَ الْأُولَىٰ وَلَسَوْفَ يُعْطِيكَ رَبُّكَ فَتَرْضَىٰ

The Prophet's own life, especially his difficult childhood, stands as a testimony to this divine commitment: "Did He not find you an orphan and give you shelter? And He found you wandering, and

He gave you guidance. And He found you in need, and made you independent." [93:6-8]

أَلَمْ يَجِدْكَ يَتِيمًا فَآوَىٰ وَوَجَدَكَ ضَالًّا فَهَدَىٰ وَوَجَدَكَ عَائِلًا فَأَغْنَىٰ

Therefore, do not doubt the help that comes from God, and do not withhold your own material or moral support from others: "Therefore, treat not the orphan with harshness, nor repulse the petitioner; but the Bounty of your Lord—rehearse and proclaim!" [93:9-11]

فَأَمَّا الْيَتِيمَ فَلَا تَقْهَرْ وَأَمَّا السَّائِلَ فَلَا تَنْهَرْ وَأَمَّا بِنِعْمَةِ رَبِّكَ فَحَدِّثْ

Chapter Seven

Quranic Expressions: A Tool to Study the Emergence of Moral Classes

Morality forms the foundation and core of Islamic teachings. The Quran does not divide society along racial, ethnic, or socio-economic lines. Instead, it seeks to establish moral classes based on the lofty values derived from the Beautiful Names of Allah, characterized by the ethical conduct and good manners of their members. Readers of the Quran are invited to join these moral classes and adopt the qualities described within them.

Moral Classes in the Quran

The Quran highlights the attributes and behaviors of various groups, such as:

the Believers (المؤمنون)

"Certainly will the believers have succeeded."

قَدْ أَفْلَحَ الْمُؤْمِنُونَ

[23:1-11]

the Praying Believers (المصلين)

"Except those who pray…"

إِلَّا الْمُصَلِّينَ

[70:22-35]

the God-conscious (المتقين)

"This is the Book about which there is no doubt, a guidance for those conscious of Allah."

ذَٰلِكَ الْكِتَابُ لَا رَيْبَ فِيهِ هُدًى لِّلْمُتَّقِينَ

[2:2-5]

the Righteous (الأبرار)

"Indeed, the righteous will drink from a cup [of wine] whose mixture is of Kafur…"

إِنَّ الْأَبْرَارَ يَشْرَبُونَ مِن كَأْسٍ كَانَ مِزَاجُهَا كَافُورًا

[76:5-10]

the Good Doers (المحسنين)

"Indeed, the righteous will be among gardens and springs…"

إِنَّ الْمُتَّقِينَ فِي جَنَّاتٍ وَعُيُونٍ

[51:15-19]

the Worshippers of the Most Merciful (عباد الرحمن)

"And the servants of the Most Merciful are those who walk upon the earth easily…"

وَعِبَادُ الرَّحْمَٰنِ الَّذِينَ يَمْشُونَ عَلَى الْأَرْضِ هَوْنًا

[25:63-76]

Progression of Virtues and Added Values

A closer examination of these moral classes reveals a progression of virtues and added values among them. The Good Doers, for example, go beyond the attributes of the Believers and Praying

Believers. They do not restrict their prayers to the obligatory ones, but rise from their beds in the night to pray and seek forgiveness:

"They used to sleep but little of the night, and in the hours before dawn they would ask forgiveness."

كَانُوا قَلِيلًا مِّنَ اللَّيْلِ مَا يَهْجَعُونَ وَبِالْأَسْحَارِ هُمْ يَسْتَغْفِرُونَ

[51:17-18]

They do not limit their charity to the obligatory Zakat:

"And those within whose wealth is a known right for the petitioner and the deprived."

وَالَّذِينَ فِي أَمْوَالِهِمْ حَقٌّ مَّعْلُومٌ لِّلسَّائِلِ وَالْمَحْرُومِ

[70:24-25]

but keep their giving open and generous:

"And from their properties was [given] the right of the [needy] petitioner and the deprived."

وَفِي أَمْوَالِهِمْ حَقٌّ لِّلسَّائِلِ وَالْمَحْرُومِ

[51:19]

Similarly, the Worshippers of the Most Merciful surpass the God-conscious and serve as their leaders or role models:

"And make us an example for the righteous."

وَاجْعَلْنَا لِلْمُتَّقِينَ إِمَامًا

[25:74]

The Righteous are described as the closest to God (المقربون):

"Indeed, the record of the righteous is in 'Illiyyun."

إِنَّ كِتَابَ الْأَبْرَارِ لَفِي عِلِّيِّينَ

[83:18-28]

The early followers of Islam, under the guidance of the Prophet (PBUH), reflected on these different attributes, believed in them, and shaped their behavior accordingly. The Quran designated these moral classes and gave them their names only after their respective qualities were manifested in real life. New habits were introduced in Mecca, and the believers practiced them consistently to acquire a new identity that would define their character. The Quranic expressions describing these moral classes became even more prominent in Medina, as the believers reached their goals and established their moral identities. Later generations were then invited to join these moral classes, which expressed their moral aspirations and ethical milestones.

Immoral Classes and Social Illnesses

On the opposite end of the moral spectrum, the Quran draws the attention of its readers to immoral classes that can corrupt society and warns believers against joining them. For example, the Dealers in Fraud (المطففين) are addressed in the Quran:

"Woe to those that deal in fraud, those who, when they have to receive by measure from men, exact full measure, but when they have to give by measure or weight to men, give less than due."

وَيْلٌ لِلْمُطَفِّفِينَ الَّذِينَ إِذَا اكْتَالُوا عَلَى النَّاسِ يَسْتَوْفُونَ وَإِذَا كَالُوهُمْ أَو وَّزَنُوهُمْ يُخْسِرُونَ

[83:1-3]

They are later described as guilty of their crime at the end of the same Surah:

"Indeed, those who committed crimes used to laugh at those who believed…"

إِنَّ الَّذِينَ أَجْرَمُوا كَانُوا مِنَ الَّذِينَ آمَنُوا يَضْحَكُونَ

[83:29-36]

The Mushrikeen (مشركين) belong to a dangerous system that divides society into different groups:

"Do not be among those who associate others with Allah, those who have divided their religion and become sects, every faction rejoicing in what it has."

وَلَا تَكُونُوا مِنَ الْمُشْرِكِينَ مِنَ الَّذِينَ فَرَّقُوا دِينَهُمْ وَكَانُوا شِيَعًا كُلُّ حِزْبٍ بِمَا لَدَيْهِمْ فَرِحُونَ

[30:31-32]

They also mislead their people, as custodians of idols, to sacrifice their children at the altar of these idols, confusing and destroying their beliefs:

"And likewise, to many of the polytheists their partners have made to seem pleasing the killing of their children in order to bring about their destruction and to confuse them in their religion."

وَكَذَلِكَ زَيَّنَ لِكَثِيرٍ مِنَ الْمُشْرِكِينَ قَتْلَ أَوْلَادِهِمْ شُرَكَاؤُهُمْ لِيُرْدُوهُمْ وَلِيَلْبِسُوا عَلَيْهِمْ دِينَهُمْ

[6:137]

The Kuffar (كفار) are those who reject the Truth and show ingratitude to God. They go further by preventing others from accepting the Truth, causing turmoil and disturbance (فتنة) in society:

"And fight them until there is no [more] fitnah and [until] worship is [acknowledged to be] for Allah. But if they cease, then there is to be no aggression except against the oppressors."

وَقَاتِلُوهُمْ حَتَّىٰ لَا تَكُونَ فِتْنَةٌ وَيَكُونَ الدِّينُ لِلَّهِ فَإِنِ انتَهَوْا فَلَا عُدْوَانَ إِلَّا عَلَى الظَّالِمِينَ

[2:190-193]

The Munafiqeen (منافقين) are not only hypocrites but also conspirators who work secretly to disrupt the fabric of society. The Quran describes them as fasiqeen (فاسقين):

"But when He gave them from His bounty, they were stingy with it and turned away while they refused."

فَلَمَّا آتَاهُم مِّن فَضْلِهِ بَخِلُوا بِهِ وَتَوَلَّوا وَّهُم مُّعْرِضُونَ

[9:76]

Their aim is to destroy every type of relationship and spread corruption and mischief on earth:

"Those who break the covenant of Allah after contracting it and sever that which Allah has ordered to be joined and cause corruption on earth. It is those who are the losers."

الَّذِينَ يَنقُضُونَ عَهْدَ اللَّهِ مِن بَعْدِ مِيثَاقِهِ وَيَقْطَعُونَ مَا أَمَرَ اللَّهُ بِهِ أَن يُوصَلَ وَيُفْسِدُونَ فِي الْأَرْضِ أُولَٰئِكَ هُمُ الْخَاسِرُونَ

[2:26-27]

All these conditions are considered social illnesses, and no one is inherently immune to them. Every human being must continuously strive to avoid the immoral behaviors associated with these groups.

Habits and the Formation of Culture

Many authors in recent years have explored the power of habit and outlined the psychological steps required to acquire specific habits. However, more than 600 years ago, Ibn Khaldun studied habits as an essential part of the science of the nature of culture, or "Imran" (عمران). Since culture is a characteristic of human beings, the nature of culture must be understood in relation to what is natural for humans. Therefore, the study of culture begins with the study and understanding of human nature.

Although intellect is the noblest faculty of humanity, human desires are innate faculties that complement the intellect. The most basic are bodily appetites, but more complex desires also exist, including—though not limited to—anger and calmness, fear and hope, affiliation, solidarity, victory, superiority, and glory.

Human faculties and desires are satisfied through activities that are performed repeatedly. The repetition of actions forms habits, and frequent repetition makes these habits deeply rooted or ingrained, becoming a second nature or habitus, known as "Malaka" (ملكة).

Two categories of habit must be recognized:

1. Habits of the arts, which are judged by the things produced—these are habits of making.

2. Habits of character, which reflect the doer—these are habits of doing.

As we can see, human actions follow patterns that are discernible to human reason. Therefore, culture can be both the subject and the objective of rational science. The science of culture is concerned with habits, as well as the natural desires and faculties that lead to them. Culture, therefore, can be defined as the totality of conventionalized habits, arts, and institutions.

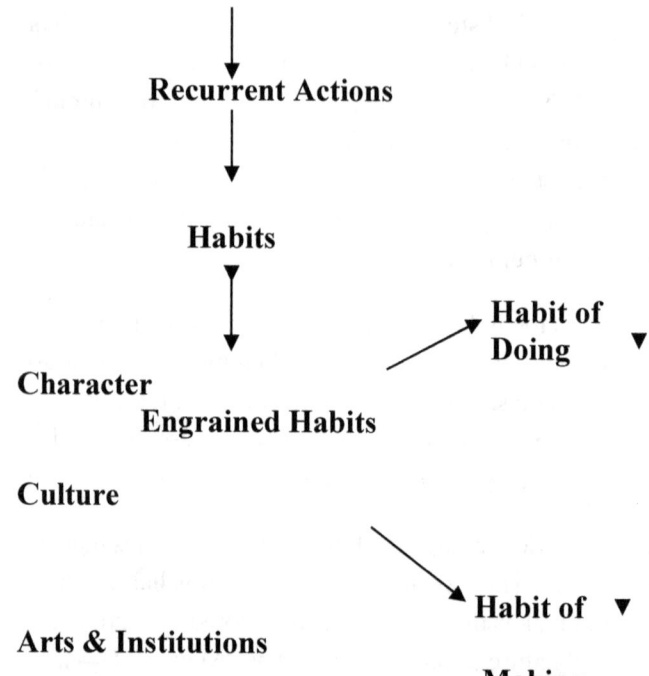

Figure 1. The role of habits in the formation of culture

The above diagram illustrates the process by which habits contribute to the formation of culture:

1. **Human Intellect + Human Desires** are the starting point.
2. These lead to **Recurrent Actions**—repeated behaviors driven by intellect and desires.
3. **Recurrent Actions** develop into **Habits** through repetition.

4. With continued practice, these become **Engrained Habits** (deeply rooted or second nature).
5. **Engrained Habits** branch into two main types:
    - **Habit of Doing**, which shapes **Character**.
    - **Habit of Making**, which leads to **Arts & Institutions**.
6. Both **Character** and **Arts & Institutions** together contribute to the formation of **Culture**.

Figure 1 visually demonstrates that culture is the result of both personal character (formed by habits of doing) and collective arts and institutions (formed by habits of making), all originating from the interplay of human intellect and desires.

The Prophetic Model of Moral Education

What system did the Prophet (PBUH) follow to instill in his followers the habits that increase their goodness and refine their character? The currently accepted educational model begins with the gathering of information as the first step. In the second step, these pieces of information are assembled to form knowledge. Finally, this knowledge is applied in real life, a stage often referred to as wisdom.

In several places, the Quran describes the mission of the Prophet as the ultimate teacher, following this same educational model. First, he would recite the verses of the Quran as units of meaning and pieces of information. These verses, however, are part of a larger construct; when combined, they form knowledge about a particular issue or provide a response to a question or challenge. The Prophet would then teach his followers how to translate this knowledge into practical application. The Quran refers to this final step as hikmah (wisdom). Wisdom is generally defined as putting everything in its proper place. The Prophet's application of knowledge was the result of the interplay between revelation (as the source of guidance and direction) and his understanding of society in its specific time, place, and circumstances.

The Quran says:

"Our Lord! Send among them a Messenger of their own who shall rehearse Your signs to them and teach them the Book and wisdom."

رَبَّنَا وَابْعَثْ فِيهِمْ رَسُولًا مِنْهُمْ يَتْلُو عَلَيْهِمْ آيَاتِكَ وَيُعَلِّمُهُمُ الْكِتَابَ وَالْحِكْمَةَ

[2:129]

However, the Quran expands this model and elevates it to a higher, more comprehensive level by adding two major components that create the right conditions for success:

"Just as We have sent among you a messenger from yourselves reciting to you Our verses and purifying you and teaching you the Book and wisdom and teaching you new knowledge."

كَمَا أَرْسَلْنَا فِيكُمْ رَسُولًا مِنكُمْ يَتْلُو عَلَيْكُمْ آيَاتِنَا وَيُزَكِّيكُمْ وَيُعَلِّمُكُمُ الْكِتَابَ وَالْحِكْمَةَ وَيُعَلِّمُكُم مَّا لَمْ تَكُونُوا تَعْلَمُونَ

[2:151]

The first component of success is tazkia (تزكية), or the increase in the goodness of the students, which is the main goal of the educational system. The foundational elements—information, knowledge, and wisdom—equip students with the tools and skills necessary to acquire the habits of various arts, enabling them to be productive, effective, and innovative members of their communities. Tazkia, on the other hand, instills in them the habits of character, or khuluq (خلق), which define students as doers and shape who they are.

Both the habits of arts and the habits of character are essential to develop new, balanced human beings—individuals who are capable of taking actions that advance civilization, while also ensuring that their actions are guided in the right direction: the direction of truth, by adhering to the high values that all stem from the Beautiful Names of Allah.

According to the Quran, both types of habits are required for true success. The daughters of Prophet Shuayb described Prophet Moses as not only strong enough to work for them, but also trustworthy:

"O my father! Hire him: truly the best of men to employ is the one who is strong and trustworthy."

يَا أَبَتِ اسْتَأْجِرْهُ إِنَّ خَيْرَ مَنِ اسْتَأْجَرْتَ الْقَوِيُّ الْأَمِينُ

[28:26]

When Prophet Yusuf recommended himself to the King of Egypt to oversee the storehouses of the kingdom, he described himself as someone who possesses both knowledge and expertise, as well as honesty and integrity:

"Appoint me over the storehouses of the land. Indeed, I will be a knowledgeable guardian."

اجْعَلْنِي عَلَى خَزَائِنِ الْأَرْضِ إِنِّي حَفِيظٌ عَلِيمٌ

[12:55]

At the heart of Surah Al-Shams (The Sun), we find a core message about the significance of the habits of character in defining the human self:

"He has succeeded who purifies it, and he has failed who instills it with corruption."

قَدْ أَفْلَحَ مَن زَكَّاهَا وَقَدْ خَابَ مَن دَسَّاهَا

[91:9-10]

Our success depends on the degree of goodness we add to ourselves and the level of self-development we achieve. We fail when we stagnate and halt our own growth and development. The word "dassaha" (دسّاها) implies burying ourselves in the dust, preventing our advancement, and causing our social death. In other words, the Quran gives us the freedom to choose between two completely opposite mindsets: the growth mindset versus the fixed or social death mindset.

The second component of success is for students in every field of knowledge to pursue what is new. This requires a deep belief in the possibilities that still lie in the unknown. The Quran considers belief in the "unknown" as the first condition for the success of the high-quality class in society, al-muttaqeen (المتقين):

"Those who believe in the unseen, establish prayer, and spend out of what We have provided for them; and who believe in what has been revealed to you, [O Muhammad], and what was revealed before you, and of the Hereafter they are certain [in faith]. Those are upon [right] guidance from their Lord, and it is those who are the successful."

$$\text{الَّذِينَ يُؤْمِنُونَ بِالْغَيْبِ وَيُقِيمُونَ الصَّلَاةَ وَمِمَّا رَزَقْنَاهُمْ يُنفِقُونَ وَالَّذِينَ يُؤْمِنُونَ بِمَا أُنزِلَ إِلَيْكَ وَمَا أُنزِلَ مِن قَبْلِكَ وَبِالْآخِرَةِ هُمْ يُوقِنُونَ أُولَٰئِكَ عَلَىٰ هُدًى مِّن رَّبِّهِمْ وَأُولَٰئِكَ هُمُ الْمُفْلِحُونَ}$$

[2:3-5]

Any educational system will yield the best results if it provides an environment where students are always encouraged to push boundaries and reach into the unknown, bringing new possibilities into the world through creativity and innovation.

"So blessed be Allah, the best of creators."

$$\text{فَتَبَارَكَ اللَّهُ أَحْسَنُ الْخَالِقِينَ}$$

[23:14]

No true creation can occur except in an environment of freedom. Those who are most grounded in knowledge are the ones who never stop their journey of liberation and keep their minds open to new knowledge and truths.

"But those among them who are well-grounded in knowledge and the believers, believe in what has been revealed to you and what was revealed before you."

$$\text{لَّٰكِنِ الرَّاسِخُونَ فِي الْعِلْمِ مِنْهُمْ وَالْمُؤْمِنُونَ يُؤْمِنُونَ بِمَا أُنزِلَ إِلَيْكَ وَمَا أُنزِلَ مِن قَبْلِكَ}$$

[4:162]

Chapter Eight

The Evolution of Umma: Quranic Expressions as a Roadmap

Is the establishment of the Umma necessary, and was the Prophet (PBUH) instrumental in this endeavor?

To answer this question, I will use a phenomenon from the universe to bring the issue closer to our understanding. One might think that the Sun creates the Day. However, according to the Quran, it is the Day that reveals the Sun:

The Sun and the Day: A Quranic Analogy

"By the Day as it shows up the Sun."

وَالنَّهَارِ إِذَا جَلَّاهَا

[91:3]

In outer space, the Sun appears as a dark disc surrounded by a thin halo, with nothing to reflect its light. On Earth, however, the light of the Sun is manifested because countless particles reflect it when the Earth faces the Sun during the Day. Thus, the creation of the Sun and the Moon requires the creation of the Day and the Night in order to fulfill their purpose of illumination:

"It is He Who created the Night and the Day, and the Sun and the Moon; all (the celestial bodies) swim along, each in its rounded course."

وَهُوَ الَّذِي خَلَقَ اللَّيْلَ وَالنَّهَارَ وَالشَّمْسَ وَالْقَمَرَ كُلٌّ فِي فَلَكٍ يَسْبَحُونَ

[21:33]

The Sun in the Quran is described as a burning lamp, "Siraj" (سراج):

"See you not how Allah has created the seven heavens one above another, and made the moon a light in their midst, and made the sun as a (Glorious) Lamp?"

أَلَمْ تَرَوْا كَيْفَ خَلَقَ اللَّهُ سَبْعَ سَمَاوَاتٍ طِبَاقًا وَجَعَلَ الْقَمَرَ فِيهِنَّ نُورًا وَجَعَلَ الشَّمْسَ سِرَاجًا

[71:15-16]

The Prophet as "Siraj"

Prophet Muhammad (PBUH) is also described in the Quran as a "Siraj":

"O Prophet! Truly We have sent you as a Witness, a Bearer of Glad Tidings, and a Warner, and as one who invites to Allah by His leave, and as a Lamp spreading Light."

يَا أَيُّهَا النَّبِيُّ إِنَّا أَرْسَلْنَاكَ شَاهِدًا وَمُبَشِّرًا وَنَذِيرًا وَدَاعِيًا إِلَى اللَّهِ بِإِذْنِهِ وَسِرَاجًا مُنِيرًا

[33:45-46]

He brought the light of the Divine Message. However, his light would not be fully appreciated until it was reflected by a community of believers around him:

"Should they intend to deceive you, verily Allah suffices you: He has strengthened you with His aid and with the Believers; and He has put affection between their hearts: if you had spent all that is in the earth, you could not have produced that affection, but Allah has done it: for He is Exalted in Might, Wise. O Prophet! Sufficient for you is Allah and for those who follow you among the Believers."

وَإِن يُرِيدُوا أَن يَخْدَعُوكَ فَإِنَّ حَسْبَكَ اللَّهُ هُوَ الَّذِي أَيَّدَكَ بِنَصْرِهِ وَبِالْمُؤْمِنِينَ وَأَلَّفَ بَيْنَ قُلُوبِهِمْ لَوْ أَنفَقْتَ مَا فِي الْأَرْضِ جَمِيعًا مَّا أَلَّفْتَ بَيْنَ قُلُوبِهِمْ وَلَٰكِنَّ اللَّهَ أَلَّفَ بَيْنَهُمْ إِنَّهُ عَزِيزٌ حَكِيمٌ يَا أَيُّهَا النَّبِيُّ حَسْبُكَ اللَّهُ وَمَنِ اتَّبَعَكَ مِنَ الْمُؤْمِنِينَ

[8:62-64]

The Meaning and Evolution of "Umma"

"Umma" (أمة) is the term used to describe such a community of believers. The establishment of the Umma with specific characteristics is, therefore, a social necessity and cannot be neglected:

"Let there arise out of you a community of people inviting to all that is good, enjoining what is right, and forbidding what is wrong: they are the ones to attain felicity."

وَلْتَكُن مِّنكُمْ أُمَّةٌ يَدْعُونَ إِلَى الْخَيْرِ وَيَأْمُرُونَ بِالْمَعْرُوفِ وَيَنْهَوْنَ عَنِ الْمُنكَرِ وَأُولَٰئِكَ هُمُ الْمُفْلِحُونَ

[3:104]

Before we explore these characteristics, let us trace the different meanings of the term "Umma" as it is used in various contexts in the Quran, in order to understand the evolution of any community in general, and the community of believers in particular.

During the journey of Moses (PBUH) to Madyan, the Quran tells us that he found an "Umma"—a group of people—drawing water from its source:

"And when he arrived at the watering (place) in Madyan, he found there a group of men watering."

وَلَمَّا وَرَدَ مَاءَ مَدْيَنَ وَجَدَ عَلَيْهِ أُمَّةً مِّنَ النَّاسِ يَسْقُونَ

[28:23]

What matters here is not the number of people, but their common goal: obtaining water. Once their goal was achieved, they dispersed, and the "Umma" ceased to exist.

In the story of Joseph (PBUH), the term "Umma" is used to refer to a specific period of time:

"But the man who had been released, one of the two (who had been in prison), and who now remembered him after a space of time…"

وَقَالَ الَّذِي نَجَا مِنْهُمَا وَادَّكَرَ بَعْدَ أُمَّةٍ

[12:45]

"Umma" is also used in the Quran to mean an idea, belief, or way of life:

"Nay! They say: We found our fathers following a certain idea, and we do guide ourselves by their footsteps. Just in the same way, whenever We sent a warner before you to any people, the wealthy ones among them said: We found our fathers following a certain idea, and we will certainly follow in their footsteps."

بَلْ قَالُوا إِنَّا وَجَدْنَا آبَاءَنَا عَلَىٰ أُمَّةٍ وَإِنَّا عَلَىٰ آثَارِهِم مُّهْتَدُونَ وَكَذَٰلِكَ مَا أَرْسَلْنَا مِن قَبْلِكَ فِي قَرْيَةٍ مِّن نَّذِيرٍ إِلَّا قَالَ مُتْرَفُوهَا إِنَّا وَجَدْنَا آبَاءَنَا عَلَىٰ أُمَّةٍ وَإِنَّا عَلَىٰ آثَارِهِم مُّقْتَدُونَ

[43:22-23]

From the above, we can identify the elements needed for the birth of an "Umma." An "Umma" is a group of people united around a common and enduring goal. It forms over time and, like individuals, it has its own lifespan:

"To every people is a term appointed: when their term is reached, not an hour can they cause delay, nor can they advance."

وَلِكُلِّ أُمَّةٍ أَجَلٌ فَإِذَا جَاءَ أَجَلُهُمْ لَا يَسْتَأْخِرُونَ سَاعَةً وَلَا يَسْتَقْدِمُونَ

[7:34]

"To every people is a term appointed."

لِكُلِّ أُمَّةٍ أَجَلٌ

[10:49]

Every "Umma" receives its appointed Messenger:

"To every people is a messenger appointed."

وَلِكُلِّ أُمَّةٍ رَّسُولٌ

[10:47]

Or a warner:

"Verily We have sent you in truth, as a bearer of glad tidings, and as a warner: and there never was a people, without a warner having lived among them."

إِنَّا أَرْسَلْنَاكَ بِالْحَقِّ بَشِيرًا وَنَذِيرًا وَإِن مِّنْ أُمَّةٍ إِلَّا خَلَا فِيهَا نَذِيرٌ

[35:24]

Each Messenger covers an era, and each era has its own Divine Reference or Book:

"For each period is a Book assigned."

لِكُلِّ أَجَلٍ كِتَابٌ

[13:38]

The current era is the era of Prophet Muhammad (PBUH), the last Prophet to humanity:

"Muḥammad is not the father of any of your men, but the Messenger of Allah, and the Seal of the Prophets: and Allah has full knowledge of all things."

مَّا كَانَ مُحَمَّدٌ أَبَا أَحَدٍ مِّن رِّجَالِكُمْ وَلَـٰكِن رَّسُولَ اللَّهِ وَخَاتَمَ النَّبِيِّينَ وَكَانَ اللَّهُ بِكُلِّ شَيْءٍ عَلِيمًا

[33:40]

And the Quran is the Book of this era.

Crisis and the Quranic Recipe for Rescue

It is fair to say that the Muslim "Umma" in particular, and the world in general, are suffering from a major crisis. This situation is not different from the diagnosis made by the Quran in the past: corruption and mischief have spread across land and sea:

"Mischief has appeared on land and sea."

ظَهَرَ الْفَسَادُ فِي الْبَرِّ وَالْبَحْرِ

[30:41]

Can the Quran intervene and provide rescue in times of crisis? Surah Al-Tariq, "The Morning Star" (الطارق), offers an excellent recipe for salvation during moments of total despair, when nothing seems to work and the "Umma" is unable to move forward to achieve its higher goals and objectives. The Surah reminds the "Umma" of God, the ultimate source of guidance. The morning star is used as a metaphor for the light of the Divine Message piercing through the darkness that surrounds the "Umma":

"By the Sky and the Night-Visitor; and what will explain to you what the Night-Visitor is? The Star of piercing brightness; there is no soul but has a protector over it."

وَالسَّمَاءِ وَالطَّارِقِ وَمَا أَدْرَاكَ مَا الطَّارِقُ النَّجْمُ الثَّاقِبُ إِنْ كُلُّ نَفْسٍ لَمَّا عَلَيْهَا حَافِظٌ

[86:1-4]

The matter is serious and requires the seriousness of the Quran and its decisive statements, which are far from any form of amusement or triviality:

"Behold, this is the Word that distinguishes (Good from Evil): It is not a thing for amusement."

إِنَّهُ لَقَوْلٌ فَصْلٌ وَمَا هُوَ بِالْهَزْلِ

[86:13-14]

The Quran is like rain descending from the sky, bringing life to dead land:

"By the Sky which returns, and by the Earth which opens out."

وَالسَّمَاءِ ذَاتِ الرَّجْعِ وَالْأَرْضِ ذَاتِ الصَّدْعِ

[86:11-12]

Prophet Muhammad (PBUH) himself must act like the thirsty land, ready to respond to the command coming from Heaven:

"Therefore expound openly what you are commanded, and turn away from those who join false gods with Allah."

فَاصْدَعْ بِمَا تُؤْمَرُ وَأَعْرِضْ عَنِ الْمُشْرِكِينَ

[15:94]

The "Umma," in turn, should follow his example and respond to the Divine Command as he did. The "Umma" must not doubt the possibility of returning and overcoming its state of despair and helplessness:

"Surely (Allah) is able to bring him back (to life)! The Day that (all) things secret will be tested, Man will have no power, and no helper."

إِنَّهُ عَلَىٰ رَجْعِهِ لَقَادِرٌ يَوْمَ تُبْلَى السَّرَائِرُ فَمَا لَهُ مِن قُوَّةٍ وَلَا نَاصِرٍ

[86:8-10]

There is no place for despair if the "Umma" believes that life is protected by God and His Angels, without which life would be impossible:

"There is no soul but has a protector over it. Now let man but think from what he is created! He is created from a drop emitted—proceeding from between the backbone and the ribs."

إِن كُلُّ نَفْسٍ لَّمَّا عَلَيْهَا حَافِظٌ فَلْيَنظُرِ الْإِنسَانُ مِمَّ خُلِقَ خُلِقَ مِن مَّاءٍ دَافِقٍ يَخْرُجُ مِن بَيْنِ الصُّلْبِ وَالتَّرَائِبِ

[86:4-7]

Why, then, should the "Umma" doubt that it will be left without Divine protection during times of moral and spiritual decline? The "Umma" must always remain vigilant and stand up to the systems of power that plot for its destruction and block its return:

"As for them, they are but plotting a scheme, and I am planning a scheme. Therefore, grant a delay to the Unbelievers: give respite to them gently."

إِنَّهُمْ يَكِيدُونَ كَيْدًا وَأَكِيدُ كَيْدًا فَمَهِّلِ الْكَافِرِينَ أَمْهِلْهُمْ رُوَيْدًا

[86:15-17]

This recipe for salvation does not work spontaneously. The members of the "Umma" are the agents of change, responsible for determining the right measures and ingredients of this recipe:

"For each (such person) there are (angels) in succession, before and behind him: they guard him by command of Allah."

لَهُ مُعَقِّبَاتٌ مِّن بَيْنِ يَدَيْهِ وَمِنْ خَلْفِهِ يَحْفَظُونَهُ مِنْ أَمْرِ اللَّهِ

[13:11]

Returning to Fitra and High Values

The first step in the revival of the "Umma" is to return to its human "Fitra" (فطرة)—the original blueprint that preceded time and history and defined what it means to be human at the moment of creation. What will the "Umma" find in "Fitra"? They will discover all the high values, "Qiam" (قيم), derived from the Eternal and Beautiful Names of God:

"So set your face firmly towards the religion, as a pure natural believer—God's original creation upon which He created mankind. There is no change in God's creation. That is the upright religion, but most people do not know."

فَأَقِمْ وَجْهَكَ لِلدِّينِ حَنِيفًا فِطْرَتَ اللَّهِ الَّتِي فَطَرَ النَّاسَ عَلَيْهَا لَا تَبْدِيلَ لِخَلْقِ اللَّهِ ذَٰلِكَ الدِّينُ الْقَيِّمُ وَلَٰكِنَّ أَكْثَرَ النَّاسِ لَا يَعْلَمُونَ

[30:30]

The new "Umma" must be founded, like the one originally raised by the Prophet, on these high values:

"You are the best community ever raised for humanity—you encourage good, forbid evil, and believe in Allah."

كُنتُمْ خَيْرَ أُمَّةٍ أُخْرِجَتْ لِلنَّاسِ تَأْمُرُونَ بِالْمَعْرُوفِ وَتَنْهَوْنَ عَنِ الْمُنكَرِ وَتُؤْمِنُونَ بِاللَّهِ

[3:110]

All these high values are summarized in one Quranic expression: "Maaruf" (معروف), meaning that which is evidently and universally known. These values are recognized and shared by all humans, everywhere and at all times. The Quran prescribes them without any qualifier—they are not labeled as Islamic, Muhammadan, Abrahamic, or Judeo-Christian. The newly born "Umma" has the responsibility to be a model in practicing and enjoining these high values in every setting, and in rejecting their opposites.

It Is noteworthy that this foundation of high values precedes even the belief In God. This indicates that an environment where high values prevail is the best condition for people to come to know God and believe in Him and His Beautiful Names. The belief in the One God, or "Tawheed" (توحيد), is not merely about the number "one," but about a vision through which believers see and understand the world.

Thus, the concept of "Tawheed" extends to include unity between husband and wife, restoring the original singular self:

"He created you (all) from a single person."

خَلَقَكُم مِّن نَّفْسٍ وَاحِدَةٍ

[39:6]

It also includes unity among the believers as one "Umma," which encompasses all the followers and disciples of all Prophets and Messengers before Prophet Muhammad (PBUT):

"Indeed, this, your religion, is one religion, and I am your Lord, so worship Me."

إِنَّ هَذِهِ أُمَّتُكُمْ أُمَّةً وَاحِدَةً وَأَنَا رَبُّكُمْ فَاعْبُدُونِ

[21:92]

"And indeed this, your religion, is one religion, and I am your Lord, so fear Me."

وَإِنَّ هَذِهِ أُمَّتُكُمْ أُمَّةً وَاحِدَةً وَأَنَا رَبُّكُمْ فَاتَّقُونِ

[23:52]

It further extends to unity among various human tribes and nations through the concept of "Taaruf" (تعارف)—notice the linguistic connection to "Maaruf"—and to the unity between humanity and the rest of the universe, as described earlier in this book.

The standard or benchmark for the newly emerging "Umma" is justice and balance, known as "Wasat" (وسط):

"And thus We have made you a just (balanced) community…"

وَكَذَلِكَ جَعَلْنَاكُمْ أُمَّةً وَسَطًا

[2:143]

The word "Kazhalika" (كذلك) at the beginning of the verse signals that what follows represents a standard or benchmark. "Wasat" literally means to be in the middle, or the Golden Median. Interestingly, this verse is physically located at the center of Surah Al-Baqara (البقرة).

How is the Golden Median achieved in the social life of the newly emerging "Umma," thus creating a model to be emulated by other nations and communities? To answer this question, we must first define the Golden Median. Individuals and communities tend to gravitate toward two diametrically opposite extremes:

The first extreme is the total rejection of the world and all its aspects. People who fall into this extreme become inactive, ineffective, and make no significant contribution to the advancement of human life. Monasticism is a clear example of this tendency. We can refer to this as "going outside the world."

The second, opposite extreme is total immersion in the world at the expense of the spiritual human dimension. The result is a community that is highly productive in material terms but lacks control over what it has earned or achieved. We can refer to this as "going into the world."

The Golden Median, or being in the middle, is not achieved by oscillating between these two extremes. Rather, it is achieved by responding to all human dimensions equally. The challenge is to be "in the world"—active, effective, and productive—while also having the capacity to "go outside the world," freeing the community not from the world itself, but from being imprisoned by it.

At the end of Surah Al-Fath, "The Victory" (الفتح), the Quran describes Prophet Muhammad (PBUH) and his disciples as the model for a balanced community:

"Muhammad is the Messenger of Allah; and those who are with him are strong against the disbelievers, (but) compassionate among each other. You see them bowing and prostrating (in prayer), seeking bounty from Allah and (His) pleasure. Their mark is on their faces from the trace of prostration. That is their description in the Torah. And their description in the Gospel is like a seed which sends forth its shoot, then makes it strong; it then becomes thick, and it stands on its own stem, delighting the sowers. So that He may enrage the disbelievers through them. Allah has promised those among them who believe and do righteous deeds forgiveness and a great reward."

مُحَمَّدٌ رَّسُولُ اللَّهِ وَالَّذِينَ مَعَهُ أَشِدَّاءُ عَلَى الْكُفَّارِ رُحَمَاءُ بَيْنَهُمْ تَرَاهُمْ رُكَّعًا سُجَّدًا يَبْتَغُونَ فَضْلًا مِنَ اللَّهِ وَرِضْوَانًا سِيمَاهُمْ فِي وُجُوهِهِم مِّنْ أَثَرِ السُّجُودِ ذَٰلِكَ مَثَلُهُمْ فِي التَّوْرَاةِ وَمَثَلُهُمْ فِي الْإِنجِيلِ كَزَرْعٍ أَخْرَجَ شَطْأَهُ فَآزَرَهُ فَاسْتَغْلَظَ فَاسْتَوَىٰ عَلَىٰ سُوقِهِ يُعْجِبُ الزُّرَّاعَ لِيَغِيظَ بِهِمُ الْكُفَّارَ وَعَدَ اللَّهُ الَّذِينَ آمَنُوا وَعَمِلُوا الصَّالِحَاتِ مِنْهُم مَّغْفِرَةً وَأَجْرًا عَظِيمًا

[48:29]

This model was also mentioned in the Torah, with a focus on the spiritual dimension. For the followers of Moses (PBUH), this aspect was crucial, as they were emerging from the bondage of slavery and "going into the world." In the Gospel, the followers of Jesus (PBUH) are reminded not to neglect this world, making every effort to be effective and productive even as they focus on spiritual elevation. The act of planting seeds and nurturing them over time is an excellent example of productivity, and also serves as a metaphor for the gradual process of building an "Umma."

The "technologies of the self" Introduced by Prophet Muhammad (PBUH) were Instrumental in balancing "going into the world" and "going outside the world." Examples include fasting and feasting during Ramadan [2:187], attending Friday prayer while also engaging in the marketplace [62:9-10], giving from one's wealth without excess [25:67], and wearing beautiful clothes, eating, and drinking without extravagance. These practices foster the balanced status of the "Umma."

In the next chapter, we will explore the different Quranic expressions for the virtue of giving, to trace the evolution of the "Umma."

Chapter Nine

Challenge and Response: Why is "Giving" a Different Expression in the Quran?

In this chapter, I will explore the concept of giving in its various expressions to shed light on the evolution of the Umma and its response to different challenges.

Throughout the Quran, there are numerous terms and expressions that convey the meaning of charity and describe the practice of giving. The spectrum ranges from recognizing the rights of the poor in the wealth of the rich, to situations where even saving may become unacceptable during times of crisis. This indicates a dynamic and dialectical relationship between the concept and practice of giving, and the social challenges and priorities that shape the form and mode of giving.

Giving as Self-Purification: The Early Challenge

The greatest challenge during the early years of the Quran's revelation was to transform the followers of the new message. Giving was introduced as a tool to increase the goodness of the individual believer:

"The one who spends his wealth to increase self-purification."

الَّذِي يُؤْتِي مَالَهُ يَتَزَكَّى

[92:18]

The term used to describe giving at this stage, "zakat" (زكاة), carries the meaning of increasing the goodness and purity of those who give and share.

Giving in Medina: Social Cohesion and Leadership

This objective remained important in the years that followed, after the new society was established in Medina. Goodness became a social requirement, and giving became one of the tools for leadership to use effectively to ensure the high quality of the new social model:

"Of their wealth take alms, that so you might purify and sanctify them; and pray on their behalf. Verily, your prayer is a source of tranquility for them."

خُذْ مِنْ أَمْوَالِهِمْ صَدَقَةً تُطَهِّرُهُمْ وَتُزَكِّيهِم بِهَا وَصَلِّ عَلَيْهِمْ إِنَّ صَلَاتَكَ سَكَنٌ لَهُمْ

[9:103]

Here, we can observe a process that unfolds in three stages:

1. Cleansing the self from the ills of stinginess and selfishness—"takhliya" (تخلية)

2. Beautifying the self by acquiring new attributes such as generosity and selflessness—"tahliya" (تحلية)

3. Realizing the effect of giving in the form of security and tranquility—"tajaliya" (تجلية)

In Medina, the terminology shifted to "sadaqa" (صدقة), which carries the connotation of truthfulness—truthfulness to Allah, His Message, and His Messenger, as well as truthfulness to the newly formed community and the protection of its fabric and cohesion. This becomes even more apparent when we consider the different groups in society who are eligible for this form of charity:

"Alms are for the poor and the needy, and those employed to administer them; for those whose hearts have been reconciled; for those in bondage and in debt; in the cause of Allah; and for the wayfarer."

إِنَّمَا الصَّدَقَاتُ لِلْفُقَرَاءِ وَالْمَسَاكِينِ وَالْعَامِلِينَ عَلَيْهَا وَالْمُؤَلَّفَةِ قُلُوبُهُمْ وَفِي الرِّقَابِ وَالْغَارِمِينَ وَفِي سَبِيلِ اللَّهِ وَابْنِ السَّبِيلِ

[9:60]

The objective here is to reduce the gap between those who have and those who have not. The groups mentioned in this verse are weak, and potentially marginalized and disenfranchised. Sadaqa and the minimum ordained portion, or "zakat" (زكاة), became tools to solidify and strengthen the fabric of society. Wealth should not circulate only among the rich:

"…so that it will not be a perpetual distribution among the rich from among you."

كَيْ لَا يَكُونَ دُولَةً بَيْنَ الْأَغْنِيَاءِ مِنكُمْ

[59:7]

Instead, wealth should be responsibly distributed to diffuse socioeconomic factors that divide society and provoke jealousy and hatred.

The intent of mentioning these groups in society is not to legislate or legitimize their permanent presence, nor to give them a fixed socioeconomic identity. The strategy is to weave connections among these groups and allow wealth and resources to circulate equitably among them. The Quran does not divide society along socioeconomic lines; it only recognizes moral classes, defining them by their high-quality attributes and values, such as "mu'minoon" (المؤمنون), "muttaqoon" (المتقون), and others.

Nifaq and Infaq: The Internal Challenge

The solidarity of the newly formed society in Medina soon became the target of a new social disease or phenomenon: nifaq (نفاق). This was an underground movement aimed at destroying the fabric of society from within. It is more accurate to refer to it as conspiracy rather than mere hypocrisy. The conspirators recognized the power of giving in strengthening the bonds of the community, so they discouraged the believers in Medina from giving to the poor and the homeless migrants who had come to Medina with the Prophet (PBUH):

"They are the ones who say, 'Do not spend on those who are with the Messenger of Allah until they disband.'"

هُمُ الَّذِينَ يَقُولُونَ لَا تُنفِقُوا عَلَىٰ مَنْ عِندَ رَسُولِ اللَّهِ حَتَّىٰ يَنفَضُّوا

[63:7]

The growing community now faced a new threat that required a new strategy. Some believers suggested to the Prophet (PBUH) that the conspirators should be physically eliminated. However, the Prophet (PBUH) understood that killing them would not solve the problem. Instead, the new strategy was to create an environment that would prevent them from growing or achieving their objectives. If the conspirators were discouraging believers from giving and sharing, the Quran's response in the same Surah was to encourage the believers to give and share:

"And spend out of what We have bestowed on you."

وَأَنفِقُوا مِمَّا رَزَقْنَاكُم

[63:10]

Notice how the language also changed. "Infaq" (إنفاق) became the new term for giving, serving as a strategy to counter "nifaq" (نفاق) and to frustrate the efforts of internal conspirators.

External Threats: Giving as Struggle

In addition to these internal conspirators, the new society also faced external enemies who threatened its safety and very existence. This challenge required a different response—a comprehensive strategy. Giving became an essential part of this strategy, supporting the fight to protect the society and preserve its mission. The language of the Quran shifted once again, matching the degree of the challenge. In such circumstances, the value of giving is considered equal to dedicating one's time, effort, and even life itself for a higher purpose:

"And struggled with their wealth and their persons in the cause of Allah."

وَجَاهَدُوا بِأَمْوَالِهِمْ وَأَنْفُسِهِمْ فِي سَبِيلِ اللَّهِ

[49:15]

Conclusion: The Dynamic Language of Giving

In conclusion, the different terms used to signify giving in the Quran change in response to the challenges faced by the believers, both as individuals and as a cohesive society. Giving is not practiced for its own sake, but as a means to achieve objectives in the social, economic, and political life of the community.

Chapter Ten

Human History: The Moral and The Morale

The essential distinguishing feature of humanity is the faculty of intellect, and reason is the foundation of human perfection. Two intellectual faculties are especially prominent in humans: discerning reason and experiential reason. Through discerning reason, human actions become intentional, ordered, and organized. Through experiential reason, humans accumulate the results of experience, deliberately choose, and transmit rules of conduct. As discussed earlier, human history is a vital component of the cosmic Quranic vision. The Quran urges its readers to travel the Earth and study the rise and fall of previous cultures and civilizations. Since the Universe serves as the reference for human action, and Revelation provides the direction for human action, history—understood as the study of human association—becomes the laboratory in which human experience is observed and tested. This process involves a two-step test:

1. The first step is to determine whether a human action was effective in the past and accepted by the Universe.
2. The second step is to confirm that the human action was guided in the right direction—the direction of Truth as depicted by Revelation.

Prophetic Guidance and Lessons from History

The Quran presents to its readers the experiences of the Prophets and Messengers, including the experience of Prophet Muhammad (PBUH) himself. The Quran urges Prophet Muhammad to follow the guidance of the Prophets who came before him:

"Those were the (prophets) who received Allah's guidance: copy the guidance they received."

أُولَٰئِكَ الَّذِينَ هَدَى اللَّهُ فَبِهُدَاهُمُ اقْتَدِهْ

[6:90]

At the same time, he is advised not to repeat an unsuccessful previous experience:

"So wait with patience for the Command of your Lord, and be not like the Companion of the Fish (Jonah)."

فَاصْبِرْ لِحُكْمِ رَبِّكَ وَلَا تَكُن كَصَاحِبِ الْحُوتِ

[68:48]

Four Functions of History in the Quran

There are four ways in which history can be utilized to produce a quality human being and a quality community:

4. A Prophet as a Model ("Uswa" أسوة):

A Prophet acts as a model for people to emulate. The Quran refers to such a model as "Uswa" (أسوة):

"You have indeed in the Messenger of Allah a beautiful pattern (of conduct) for anyone whose hope is in Allah and the Final Day, and who engages much in the praise of Allah."

لَقَدْ كَانَ لَكُمْ فِي رَسُولِ اللَّهِ أُسْوَةٌ حَسَنَةٌ لِّمَن كَانَ يَرْجُو اللَّهَ وَالْيَوْمَ الْآخِرَ وَذَكَرَ اللَّهَ كَثِيرًا

[33:21]

"There is for you an excellent example (to follow) in Abraham and those with him."

قَدْ كَانَتْ لَكُمْ أُسْوَةٌ حَسَنَةٌ فِي إِبْرَاهِيمَ وَالَّذِينَ مَعَهُ

[60:4]

2. A Source of Morale:

The historical accounts preserved in the Quran serve to increase the morale of the believers, especially in times of crisis:

"All that We relate to you of the stories of the messengers, with it We make firm your heart."

وَكُلًّا نَّقُصُّ عَلَيْكَ مِنْ أَنبَاءِ الرُّسُلِ مَا نُثَبِّتُ بِهِ فُؤَادَكَ

[11:120]

3. A Source of Moral "Ibra" (عبرة):

Historical accounts provide lessons to be learned, as seen in the detailed and varied experience of Prophet Joseph (PBUH):

"There is, in their stories, instruction for men endued with understanding."

لَقَدْ كَانَ فِي قَصَصِهِمْ عِبْرَةٌ لِأُولِي الْأَلْبَابِ

[12:111]

4. Transforming History into a Sign ("Ayah" آية):

The Quran transforms historical accounts into signs ("Ayah"). In Surah Al-Shuara, the Quran ends each historical account or prophetic experience with these recurring verses:

"Verily in this is a Sign: but most of them do not believe. And verily your Lord is He, the Exalted in Might, Most Merciful."

إِنَّ فِي ذَٰلِكَ لَآيَةً وَمَا كَانَ أَكْثَرُهُم مُّؤْمِنِينَ وَإِنَّ رَبَّكَ لَهُوَ الْعَزِيزُ الرَّحِيمُ

[26:68-69]

History as a Laboratory and the Quranic Approach

The objective of the Quran is to liberate its readers from the prison of systems of power—whether political, military, or economic. The Quran does not present time as a series of dates, but rather as a sequence of events and happenings. For example, although the Quran alludes to the Prophet and his companion, Abu Bakr, in the cave during their hijra, the verse was not revealed immediately after the hijra. Instead, it was revealed years later, when the Muslim community was facing tremendous hardship and severe conditions, and needed a reminder.

At that time, the Prophet and his companions were preparing for a campaign to protect Medina from an impending attack. This was known as the "campaign of hardship" because of the scarcity of provisions and the harsh weather conditions. The "campaign of hardship" became a campaign for the believers to overcome adversity and support the Prophet at a critical moment in his mission. Only when the believers developed confidence in themselves could they go forth to face the rest of the world.

At this crucial moment, the Quran reminded the community that Allah would help them just as He had helped their Prophet during the hijra:

"If you do not help him, Allah has already helped him when those who disbelieved had driven him out (of Mecca) as one of two, when they were in the cave and he said to his companion, 'Do not grieve; indeed Allah is with us.'"

إِلَّا تَنصُرُوهُ فَقَدْ نَصَرَهُ اللَّهُ إِذْ أَخْرَجَهُ الَّذِينَ كَفَرُوا ثَانِيَ اثْنَيْنِ إِذْ هُمَا فِي الْغَارِ إِذْ يَقُولُ لِصَاحِبِهِ لَا تَحْزَنْ إِنَّ اللَّهَ مَعَنَا

[9:40]

It is evident how the Quran utilizes historical events, transforming them into signs (Ayah) and lessons (Ibra), so that believers can see new possibilities and renewed hope for change when everything else seems to fail.

Surah Al-Rum: A Case Study in History and Morale

One of the most striking examples of the Quran using history for both moral and morale is the revelation of Surah Al-Rum (The Romans) in Mecca. A deep dive into Surah Al-Rum in our own time gives the attentive reader the impression that the Surah is being revealed in the twenty-first century CE, rather than in the seventh century CE. This impression reinforces the fact that the Quran is alive and fully capable of responding to the questions and challenges raised at any time or place, from the moment of its revelation until the Day of Judgment.

Let us examine the geopolitical conditions of the world at the time of the revelation of Surah Al-Rum, as well as the social and political dynamics that prevailed in Mecca when the Surah was revealed.

There was a clear power struggle between two great civilizations: the Roman and the Persian Empires. Together, these two empires dominated the world for over 1,100 years. The Roman Empire ruled over Syria and Palestine, and to the west, over Constantinople and Rome. The Persian Empire controlled the Near East, mainly present-day Iraq and Iran. Arabia, due to its harsh climate and scarce resources, was of little interest to either empire. They managed any threats from Arabia through their Arab proxies: the Romans supported their Arab allies to the north and west, Banu Ghassan, while the Persians supported their Arab allies to the east and south, Banu Lakhm.

Beginning in 54 BCE, the two empires fought each other for 600 years, resulting in the destruction of towns, fortifications, and provinces. Their final war occurred in the seventh century CE, between 602 and 628. The Hijra of the Prophet (PBUH) took place in 622 CE, according to historical records and archaeological findings. Surah Al-Rum was revealed in Mecca in 615, seven years before the Hijra. The revelation of this Surah occurred during the latter part of the Meccan period and announced the news that the Romans had been defeated in Syria and Palestine:

"The Romans have been defeated. In the nearest land."

غُلِبَتِ الرُّومُ فِي أَدْنَى الْأَرْضِ

[30:2-3]

The social and political conditions in Mecca were no better. The conflict between the Prophet (PBUH) and his small group of followers on one side, and the elites of Mecca on the other, had reached a critical point. The believers were harassed, tortured, driven out of their homes, and even executed. The risk was especially high for the most vulnerable in society, such as women, the poor, and the enslaved. The oligarchy of Mecca even plotted against the Prophet (PBUH) himself—to restrain him, to kill him, or to evict him. The Quran records their attempts:

"And remember when those who disbelieved plotted against you to restrain you, or kill you, or evict you."

وَإِذْ يَمْكُرُ بِكَ الَّذِينَ كَفَرُوا لِيُثْبِتُوكَ أَوْ يَقْتُلُوكَ أَوْ يُخْرِجُوكَ

[8:30]

Injustice and corruption prevailed not only in Mecca, but had spread to encompass the entire world—on land and at sea. The

Surah summarizes the global conditions and the state of those responsible:

"But those who unjustly follow their desires without knowledge."

بَلِ اتَّبَعَ الَّذِينَ ظَلَمُوا أَهْوَاءَهُم بِغَيْرِ عِلْمٍ

[30:29]

"Corruption has appeared throughout the land and sea by what the hands of people have earned."

ظَهَرَ الْفَسَادُ فِي الْبَرِّ وَالْبَحْرِ بِمَا كَسَبَتْ أَيْدِي النَّاسِ

[30:41]

The conditions today are very similar. Only the names and the geography have changed, but the terminology of East and West persists. The polarization between East and West still exists. The economic gap between the world powers and the rest of the world remains unchanged. Many intellectuals, overwhelmed by the power of present superpowers, believe that the survival of poorer countries depends on their allegiance to one of these superpowers.

Surah Al-Rum begins with very important news:

"The Romans have been defeated in a land close by."

غُلِبَتِ الرُّومُ فِي أَدْنَى الْأَرْضِ

[30:2-3]

The Meccans—both believers and non-believers—could not believe it. How could such a great empire be defeated? The Meccans had multiple contacts with this empire during their summer trade journeys to Syria in the north:

"Securing their journeys by Winter and Summer."

رِحْلَةَ الشِّتَاءِ وَالصَّيْفِ

[106:2]

They had seen the urban cities and towns, and the advanced social and economic life of the Romans:

"They were stronger than them: they tilled the soil, built it, and populated it more than they have done."

كَانُوا أَشَدَّ مِنْهُمْ قُوَّةً وَأَثَارُوا الْأَرْضَ وَعَمَرُوهَا أَكْثَرَ مِمَّا عَمَرُوهَا

[30:9]

They were well aware of the political and military power of the Romans. It is no wonder they were shocked by these new geopolitical developments. Nonetheless, the Romans were defeated by another world power, the Persian Empire.

At this juncture, the Surah makes a prediction:

"But they, after their defeat, will soon be victorious in a few years."

وَهُم مِّن بَعْدِ غَلَبِهِمْ سَيَغْلِبُونَ فِي بِضْعِ سِنِينَ

[30:3-4]

What is more important than the prediction itself is the message behind it:

"The Command is with Allah, before and after."

لِلَّهِ الْأَمْرُ مِن قَبْلُ وَمِن بَعْدُ

[30:4]

Everything that happens in this world—past, present, or future—is under the command and control of God. The decisions of victory and defeat are under His direct order:

"He makes victorious whom He wills, and He is the Exalted in Might, the Merciful."

يَنصُرُ مَن يَشَاءُ وَهُوَ الْعَزِيزُ الرَّحِيمُ

[30:5]

He is Al-Aziz, the Ever-Powerful—nothing can prevent His command from being fulfilled. At the same time, He is Al-Raheem, the Ever-Merciful—the believers must never doubt the mercy of Allah, and despair must not enter their hearts:

"Never give up hope of the Mercy of God. Truly, no one despairs of the Mercy of God except those who have no faith."

وَلَا تَيْأَسُوا مِن رَّوْحِ اللَّهِ إِنَّهُ لَا يَيْأَسُ مِن رَّوْحِ اللَّهِ إِلَّا الْقَوْمُ الْكَافِرُونَ

[12:87]

In fact, the prediction was realized in less than ten years. Two years after the Hijra, the Romans defeated the Persians, and by 628 CE, they had consolidated their victory. Around the same time, another pivotal event took place in Arabia: the Prophet (PBUH) and his small group of followers defeated a much larger army of the Meccan elites at the Battle of Badr. The believers rejoiced—not just because the Romans defeated the Persians, but because they themselves were granted victory. The prediction of their own triumph was fulfilled in less than ten years after the revelation of the Surah:

"On that day shall the believers rejoice because of the victory of Allah."

وَيَوْمَئِذٍ يَفْرَحُ الْمُؤْمِنُونَ بِنَصْرِ اللَّهِ

[30:4-5]

The day of the Battle of Badr was a significant milestone in the biography of the Prophet (PBUH), marking a clear division between two distinct eras—before and after. The Quran refers to it as the "Day of the Criterion":

"The Day of the Criterion."

يَوْمَ الْفُرْقَانِ

[8:41]

The promised victory extended beyond Badr. In the context of an empire being defeated, the believers received the message that they, too, could become victors on a global scale. However, this would require tremendous effort and sacrifice. The first step on the path to victory was to liberate themselves from the prison of the "superpower" mentality and from the grip of political, economic, and military power. All the statements recited to them from the beginning of Surah Al-Rum reinforce this message of liberation:

"The Command is with God, before and after."

لِلَّهِ الْأَمْرُ مِن قَبْلُ وَمِن بَعْدُ

[30:4]

"He makes victorious whom He will."

يَنصُرُ مَن يَشَاءُ

[30:5]

"It is the promise of God; never does God depart from His promise."

وَعْدَ اللَّهِ لَا يُخْلِفُ اللَّهُ وَعْدَهُ

[30:6]

If the believers—then or at any time—fail to take this first step toward victory and instead behave like a superpower, imitating their opponents, they undermine their own purpose.

The believers in Mecca at the time of the revelation of Surah Al-Rum, as well as its readers in every generation, must come to this conclusion: God is not only the Creator of the universe and humanity, but He is also in total command and control of all existence. Superpowers may use their might to oppress and destroy other nations and communities, but their power is temporary and fleeting. Indeed, the Romans were defeated—demonstrating that it can happen to anyone, even empires.

Although the Muslim community in the seventh century CE had limited power and resources and initially stood at the fringes of world politics, they were able to defeat both the Roman and Persian superpowers in a relatively short period of time, fulfilling a strategic prediction:

"On that day shall the believers rejoice because of the victory of God."

وَيَوْمَئِذٍ يَفْرَحُ الْمُؤْمِنُونَ بِنَصْرِ اللَّهِ

[30:4-5]

Epilogue

The Imperative of a Science of Guidance

Humanity's transformative progress over five centuries—powered by technologies that elevated human welfare—stemmed from a paradigm shift: abandoning Aristotelian speculation for empirical scientific methodology. This methodology anchors truth in observable reality, using the universe to validate human understanding while rejecting non-falsifiable claims.

Yet recent decades revealed a critical void. Leading philosophers, primarily in the United States, shifted epistemology's focus from 'How do we know?' to 'What do you mean?'—forcing a reckoning with the purpose and direction of human action. Who defines this trajectory?

The Quran answers this as hudá (guidance), positioning Itself as a compass for human endeavor (Quran 2:120) without negating complementary frameworks like constitutions or social traditions (Quran 17:09). For its students, the challenge lies in developing a rigorous methodology to derive this guidance systematically—a gap addressed by Dr. Neji's proposal: 'Ilm al-Wajhah (The Science of Guidance).

The Foundations of a New Discipline

Establishing a science demands more than compilation; it requires an epistemological architecture resolving interconnected disciplinary questions. The Quran's structure is foundational:
• Its smallest semantic unit, the ayah (verse), must be interpreted holistically—not as fragmented words—but as a complete idea.
• Each ayah gains deeper meaning within its surah (chapter) and the Quran's totality (Quran 75:18).

Classical scholars categorized its language into:
• Manṭūq al-Qur'ān (Signifiers): Finite textual expressions.
• Mafhūm al-Qur'ān (Signified): Infinite layers of meaning (Quran

18:109).

To navigate this, the Quran provides al-taṣdīq wa al-haymanah (Authentication and Overarching)—a methodology elevating understanding by confirming truths while transcending limitations. This mirrors prophecy's unified arc: a progressive revelation culminating in the Seal, Muhammad (PBUH) (Quran 33:40). Jesus (PBUH), for instance, authenticated the Torah while heralding Muhammad's advent (Quran 61:6). The Quran thus integrates prior revelations into a higher horizon, addressing humanity's evolving needs.

The Living Scripture and Its Future

The Quran endures as our era's vital scripture. Each generation's engagement yields new readings—but interpretations risk irrelevance if they ignore emerging challenges. When stagnation threatens, fresh readings must overarch prior understandings without negating them. This dynamism embodies the Quran's essence: a text of infinite renewal (Quran 75:19).

Its nomenclature unlocks a tripartite vision synthesizing:
1. Revelation (Divine communication),
2. The Universe (observable creation),
3. The Human (purposeful agency).

The beautiful Names of God (al-Asmā' al-Ḥusnā) anchor this vision's epistemology. Yet realizing ʿIlm al-Wajhah demands:
• A unified theory of the triad,
• Elucidation of key concepts (e.g., hudá, tadabbur),
• Innovative methods to derive principles, theories, and applications.

Future scholarship must pioneer this work—ensuring the Quran's guidance illuminates every era of humanity's journey.

Glossary of Key Terms

Term	Arabic (Script)	Definition
Fiʻl	فعل	Action; the foundational unit of human agency in the Quranic vision.
Wijha	وجهة	Direction; the orientation or purpose guiding human action.
Qibla	قبلة	Ultimate goal; the spiritual or existential focus of one's life.
Hudā	هدى	Guidance; divine direction provided by revelation.
Tawjīh	توجيه	Ethical orientation; the process of aligning actions with moral principles.
Ṣalah	صلاة	Prayer; ritual worship and spiritual connection with God.
Ṭawāf	طواف	Circumambulation; ritual act performed around the Kaʻba.
Umma	أمة	Community; a group united by shared purpose and values.
Ayah	آية	Sign or verse; the smallest semantic unit in the Quran, signifying meaning.
Sadaqa	صدقة	Voluntary charity; giving for the sake of social cohesion and truthfulness.

Zakat	زكاة	Obligatory alms; purifying wealth through required giving.
Infaq	إنفاق	Spending; the act of giving, especially in response to social challenges.
Fitra	فطرة	Innate disposition; the original human nature as created by God.
Tawheed	توحيد	Divine unity; the oneness of God and the vision of unity in creation.
Wasat	وسط	The Golden Median; balance and justice in individual and communal life.
Maaruf	معروف	That which is universally recognized as good and just.
Taaruf	تعارف	Mutual recognition; the process of knowing and connecting with others.
Ibra	عبرة	Moral lesson; insight or instruction drawn from historical accounts.
Uswa	أسوة	Model or example; a pattern of conduct to be emulated.

Note: This glossary is not exhaustive. Readers are encouraged to consult the main text for further contextual explanations and to deepen their engagement with the Quranic terminology.

Names and Expressions of the Glorious Quran:

An Interpretive Analysis

The Quran's Cosmic Vision in the Thought of Dr. Neji Ben Hadj Tahar Mzoughi

Selective Translation and Adaptation by Dr. Walid Fayez Khayr

Dedication

To those who are open to new possibilities, yet remain steadfast in the direction of truth and justice.

References

1. القرآن الكريم

    The Holy Quran.

2. **Yusuf Ali.** *The Holy Qur'an: Text, Translation and Commentary.*

3. ابن عاشور **(Ibn 'Ashur).** (التحرير والتنوير)*Al-Tahrir wa al-Tanwir*).

4. **Fazlur Rahman.** *Major Themes of the Qur'an.* University of Chicago Press, 1980.

5. مالك بن نبي **(Malek Bennabi).** (الظاهرة القرآنية)*Al-Zahirah al-Qur'aniyyah*).

6. **Jonathan Swift.** *Gulliver's Travels.* (First published 1726.)

7. **Sir Muhammad Iqbal.** *The Reconstruction of Religious Thought in Islam.* Oxford University Press, 1930.

8. **George Lakoff & Mark Johnson.** *Philosophy in the Flesh: The Embodied Mind and Its Challenge to Western Thought.* Basic Books, 1999.

9. كشف (**Muhyiddin Ibn 'Arabi**). محيي الدين ابن العربي (*Kashf al-Ma'na 'an Sir Asma' Allah al-Husna*). المعنى عن سر أسماء الله الحسنى

10. ابن الهيثم (**Ibn al-Haytham**). كتاب المناظر (*Kitab al-Manazir*).

11. المقدمة (**Ibn Khaldun**). عبد الرحمن ابن خلدون (*Al-Muqaddimah*).

12. السيوطي (**Al-Suyuti**). علوم القرآن (*'Ulum al-Qur'an*).

13. ناجي بن الحاج الطاهر المزوغي (**Neji Ben Hadj Tahar Mzoughi**). الإنسان والقرآن: معالم علم الوجهة (*Man and the Quran: An Introduction to The Science of Guidance*). دار الفكر، دمشق.

    (Original Arabic edition, source of the present translation and adaptation.)

www.ingramcontent.com/pod-product-compliance
Lightning Source LLC
Chambersburg PA
CBHW060511030426
42337CB00015B/1843